Navigating the Heartache

Understanding and Coping With Pet Loss Grief

Ellie Bloom

Contents

CHAPTER ONE

Introduction

In the quiet corners of our hearts, where love and companionship intertwine, a profound connection exists that transcends words. It is a bond forged not in shared language or common interests but in the silent symphony of understanding and unconditional love. This is the sacred union between humans and their pets, a relationship that brings immeasurable joy, laughter, and warmth into our lives. Yet, it is also a connection that, when severed, leaves behind a chasm of grief that echoes in the recesses of our souls.

I know this grief intimately, as many of you do. It is a grief that develops from the profound loss of a beloved furry friend—a loss that goes beyond the mere absence of a pet but extends into the depths of our emotional landscapes. In the following pages, I invite you to embark on a journey of solace and understanding as we explore the unique and often underestimated pain that accompanies the departure of our cherished companions.

My own story echoes the sentiments of countless pet owners who have felt the sting of this particular grief. It was a sunny afternoon when I first laid eyes on my furry confidant, a ball of fur with twinkling eyes and a heart full of immeasurable affection. Together, we navigated life, sharing laughter in moments of joy and offering comfort in times of sorrow. Our days were woven together with the threads of loyalty, companionship, and an unspoken language that only those who have loved and lost a pet can truly understand.

As the years unfolded, my dog became more than just a companion; she became an integral part of my identity, a silent witness to the years of my life. Yet, as fate would have it, the day arrived when I had to bid farewell to my loyal friend. The pain that followed was profound, a whirlwind of emotions that tore through my being, leaving me lost in my sorrow. In that moment of heartache, I realized the need for a guiding light, a source of comfort that understood the delicate intricacies of losing my beloved pet.

And so, this book emerges from this world of shared experiences, a testament to the profound and unique grief accompanying the loss of a pet. The aim is to offer solace in the shared narratives of loss and provide practical coping strategies that guide you through the maze of emotions. Together, we will navigate the ebb and flow of grief, acknowledging these waves while finding ways to honor the legacy of our dearly departed companions.

The following chapters will delve into the emotions accompanying pet loss—from the initial shock to the lingering ache of absence. We will explore the misconceptions surrounding grief over pets and challenge societal norms that may attempt to diminish the intensity of our sadness. Through the comforting embrace of shared stories and the gentle guidance of empathetic words, we will create a space where your grief is validated and understood.

Additionally, this book aims to be a practical companion in your journey through grief. From memorializing your pet's legacy to navigating the complexities of guilt and self-care, we will provide a toolkit of coping strategies tailored to the unique challenges of pet loss. While we cannot erase the pain, we can walk hand in hand, offering support and understanding as you navigate this uncharted terrain.

As you turn the pages of this book, know that you are not alone. Your grief is valid, your pain is acknowledged, and your journey is shared. Together, we will embark on a healing voyage, honoring the love that transcends time and space. May these words serve as a comforting balm for your wounded soul, guiding you through the shadows of grief and into the gentle embrace of fond memories.

CHAPTER TWO

The Unique Bond Between Pets and People

We will delve into the sacred connection that binds humans and their pets. It is a heartwarming exploration of the unique and profound bond we share with our furry companions—a bond that transcends the ordinary and fills the spaces of our lives with unconditional love, companionship, and joyous shared moments. Join me as we navigate the pages of this chapter, celebrating the extraordinary threads woven between us and our beloved pets, a bond that stands as a testament to the beauty of this connection and the profound impact these precious beings have on the human heart.

The Psychology of Pet Attachment

When it comes to human emotions and relationships, few attachments are as delicate and enduring as the bond we share with our pets. To understand the profound significance of this connection, we must look into the realm of psychology, where the complex interplay of emotions, attachment, and companionship unfolds.

The deeply ingrained human need for companionship is at the heart of our connection with pets. As social beings, we are wired to seek connections that fulfill our emotional needs, and pets, with their unwavering loyalty and non-judgmental presence, become natural companions. The mere act of petting a cat, playing fetch with a dog, or listening to the rhythmic purring of a contented feline releases a surge of oxytocin, the "love hormone," fostering a sense of connection and well-being.

Moreover, pets provide a unique form of social support. In moments of joy, sorrow, or solitude, they stand by our side, offering a steadfast presence extending beyond words. Sharing our lives with a pet creates a mutually beneficial relationship, a give-and-take of emotions that nurtures a sense of belonging and purpose. Research has shown that the presence of pets can alleviate stress, reduce feelings of loneliness, and contribute to an overall improvement in mental health.

The concept of pets as family members reflects a profound shift in societal attitudes towards these furry companions. No longer relegated to the periphery of family life, pets have firmly taken their place as integral household members. This paradigm shift can be attributed, in part, to the changing dynamics of modern living. As familial structures evolve, with more individuals living alone or in smaller households, pets fill the void, offering companionship and a sense of purpose.

The familial bond with pets is deeply rooted in the psychological phenomenon known as attachment. Just as infants form strong attachments to their caregivers, humans form deep emotional bonds with their pets. The sense of security, comfort, and unconditional love that pets provide fosters a secure attachment, creating a haven for emotional expression and connection.

Pets, in many ways, become extensions of our identity. The shared experiences, routines, and rituals we create with them contribute to a sense of continuity and stability in our lives. Whether it's the daily walk with a canine companion or the quiet moments of companionship with a cat nestled in our lap, these shared activities become crucial to our daily existence, shaping our sense of self.

Furthermore, the anthropomorphism of pets—attributing human-like qualities and emotions to them—plays a crucial role in the familial bond. When we perceive our pets as sentient beings capable of love, joy, and understanding, it deepens the emotional connection and reinforces their status as family members. This anthropomorphic lens allows us to bridge the communication gap between species, fostering a shared language of gestures, expressions, and emotions.

The significance of pets as family members is also underscored by the evolving nature of societal values. In an era where the traditional definition of family expands to encompass diverse structures, including pets as valued members, it acknowledges the varied forms that love and companionship can take. The term "fur babies" is not merely a whimsical phrase; it encapsulates a profound shift in our perception of the familial unit.

The psychology behind our connection with pets is a rich relationship of attachment, companionship, and shared identity. As family members, pets offer a unique form of social support, emotional security, and unconditional love that enriches the human experience. The significance of this bond is a testament to the power of the connection between humans and our pets.

The Role of Pets in Our Lives

Pets, those delightful companions of fur, feathers, or scales, play many roles in our lives, enriching our existence in ways far beyond the simplistic label of mere "animals." These remarkable beings assume roles that touch the very core of our emotions, well-being, and daily routines.

At the most fundamental level, pets often serve as unwavering sources of companionship. In a world that can sometimes feel chaotic and unpredictable, the constant presence of a pet provides a sense of solace and reassurance. Whether it's a purring cat curled up on a windowsill or a loyal dog waiting eagerly by the door, pets offer a consistent and dependable presence in our lives. This companionship is not contingent on success or failure, wealth or poverty; it is a steadfast connection rooted in the simple joy of shared moments.

Beyond companionship, pets frequently assume the role of emotional support providers. The intuitive understanding that pets seem to possess is nothing short of remarkable. They detect our moods with uncanny accuracy, responding to joy with exuberant play and offering a comforting presence in times of sorrow. The non-judgmental nature of this emotional support creates a safe space for authentic expression, allowing us to be vulnerable without fear of criticism or misunderstanding.

In the realm of mental health, the roles pets play are increasingly recognized and celebrated. Numerous studies have highlighted the positive impact of pet ownership on mental well-being. The act of stroking a pet, playing with them, or simply enjoying their company triggers the release of oxytocin and endorphins. These chemicals promote feelings of happiness and reduce stress. Pets become silent healers, providing a natural antidote to the pressures and anxieties caused by modern life.

The physical benefits of pet ownership are not to be underestimated. Dogs, in particular, encourage regular exercise through daily walks and play. The physical activity associated with caring for pets contributes to a healthier lifestyle, reducing the risk of cardiovascular diseases and obesity. Moreover, the routine and responsibility of pet care instill a sense of purpose, structure, and regularity in our lives.

In families, pets often assume the role of playmates and confidants, especially for children. The bonds formed with pets during childhood can impact a person's ability to empathize, communicate, and form relationships in adulthood. The lessons of responsibility and compassion learned through pet ownership become foundational building blocks for character development.

Pets can also play a crucial role in providing a sense of security. With their keen senses, dogs serve as vigilant guardians, offering both a deterrent to potential threats and a comforting presence in the home. The bond between a pet and its owner creates a unique form of protection, a silent pact that goes beyond the physical and extends into emotional security.

For those facing health challenges or living in isolation, pets become invaluable companions, offering emotional support and a reason to get out of bed each day. The unconditional love and acceptance that pets provide can be particularly transformative for individuals dealing with chronic illnesses, disabilities, or mental health disorders.

In the broader context of society, pets contribute to community well-being. They serve as social promoters, aiding interactions among neighbors and developing a sense of shared responsibility. Pet owners often form close-knit communities founded on a common love for their furry friends. This communal aspect of pet ownership strengthens social ties and creates support networks.

In essence, pets' roles in our lives are as diverse and nuanced as the relationships we share with them. From companionship and emotional support to physical well-being and community building, pets have become integral to our existence. As we open our homes and hearts to these extraordinary beings, we find ourselves not merely caring for animals but engaging in a reciprocal understanding and shared experiences that enhance our lives.

A Story of Love and Companionship

In the quiet corner of a small town, nestled between rolling hills and a meandering river, lived an elderly couple, Mr. and Mrs. Anderson. Their quaint cottage exuded warmth, echoing with the gentle hum of a well-lived life. But the true heartbeat of their home was a weathered old Labrador named Charlie.

Charlie had been a part of the Anderson family for as long as anyone could remember. He arrived as a lively puppy, full of boundless energy and an insatiable curiosity. As the years unfolded, he grew into a wise and loyal companion, his graying muzzle a testament to the passage of time.

A heavy sadness settled over the Andersons one autumn evening as they received news of Mrs. Anderson's ailing health. The weight of uncertainty loomed, and the once-vibrant home felt subdued. Sensing the shift in the atmosphere, Charlie became a constant shadow to Mrs. Anderson, his comforting presence offering solace in the face of impending change.

As Mrs. Anderson's health declined, her days became a series of quiet moments punctuated by Charlie's gentle companionship. He lay by her side, his soulful eyes reflecting an understanding that transcended words. Amid medical appointments and hushed conversations, Charlie remained a steadfast source of comfort, his head resting on her lap as if to say, "I'm here with you."

One evening, as the sun dipped below the horizon and the air turned chilly, Mrs. Anderson was too weak to move from her favorite chair by the window. Charlie, ever attuned to her needs, padded over and nuzzled her hand. In that silent exchange, a lifetime of shared memories flowed between them—the laughter of sunny afternoons, the joy of long walks, and the comfort found in each other's presence.

In the final days, as Mrs. Anderson's room filled with the soft glow of a bedside lamp, Mr. Anderson observed the profound connection between his wife and Charlie. It was as if the aging Labrador had become a bridge between this world and the next, offering a tangible link to their shared memories and love.

On the day Mrs. Anderson passed away, the house echoed with a poignant stillness. Charlie, ever vigilant, sat by the empty chair, his gaze fixed on the door as if waiting for her return. In the days that followed, grief hung heavy in the air, a palpable presence that touched every corner of the cottage.

Yet, in sorrow, a quiet transformation occurred. Mr. Anderson, now navigating the solitude that accompanied his loss, found an unexpected companion in Charlie. Having endured grief alongside his humans, the aging Labrador became a source of resilience and unwavering loyalty.

In this small town, the tale of Mr. Anderson and Charlie became a testament to the true depth of human-pet relationships. It spoke of a connection that transcends the boundaries of words, a bond that accompanies us through the seasons of life, offering solace, understanding, and a timeless reminder that love, in its purest form, knows no boundaries—not even those set by the hands of time.

The Impact of Pet Loss

The loss of a pet, seemingly a small chapter in the grand narrative of life, profoundly impacts the emotional and physical well-being of individuals. The bond between a human and their pet transcends the mundane; it is a unique and deeply emotional connection that, when severed, leaves an indelible mark on one's existence.

Emotionally, the impact of pet loss is akin to the rupture of a vital emotional artery. The grief experienced is complex and multifaceted, often catching individuals off guard with its intensity. The emotional contours of this grief journey encompass a spectrum of emotions, ranging from the initial shock and denial to the deep well of sorrow that follows. The profound sense of loss is not only for the pet's physical presence but also for the companionship, unconditional love, and the unique language of understanding shared between humans and animals.

One of the distinctive aspects of pet loss is the disenfranchised grief that often accompanies it. Society, to a large extent, has yet to fully grasp the depth of the human-animal bond and the profound impact that losing a pet can have. Well-meaning friends and family may offer condolences, but the intensity of the grief may be met with raised eyebrows or dismissive comments. This lack of acknowledgment can exacerbate the emotional toll, leaving the grieving individual feeling isolated in their sorrow.

The routine disruptions that follow pet loss further intensify the emotional impact. The simple acts of feeding, walking, and caring for a pet create a rhythm in daily life. The sudden absence of these routines can leave a void that permeates every aspect of the day. The silence where once there were playful barks or gentle purrs becomes a poignant reminder of the emptiness left behind.

In many cases, the grief experienced after losing a pet can be a unique form of anticipatory grief. As pets age, their human companions often find themselves mentally preparing for the inevitable. However, the emotional intensity can be surprising when the loss finally occurs. The anticipatory grief, rather than lessening the impact, may serve as a precursor to a cascade of complex emotions, including guilt, sadness, and a deep sense of loss.

The physical toll of pet loss is not to be underestimated. The bond between humans and their pets often extends into physical activities such as walking, playing, and general caregiving. The sudden end of these activities can lead to decreased physical exercise, disrupt established routines, and impact overall well-being. The stress associated with grief can manifest physically, contributing to sleep disturbances, changes in appetite, and a compromised immune system.

Research has indicated that the stress of losing a pet can have measurable effects on cardiovascular health. The emotional burden carried by the bereaved may manifest as palpitations, chest tightness, or other symptoms that mirror the emotional weight of grief. The interconnection between emotional and physical well-being becomes starkly apparent, emphasizing the holistic impact of pet loss on an individual.

Navigating the aftermath of pet loss requires a nuanced understanding of the intertwining threads of emotional and physical well-being. The healing process is unique to each individual, marked by the ebb and flow of grief. Acknowledging the profound impact of pet loss is critical in fostering a compassionate environment that supports those struggling with this unique form of grief.

The loss of a pet resonates far beyond the visible contours of sorrow. It ripples through the emotional landscape, leaving an enduring imprint on the hearts of those who have loved and lost. By recognizing the complex relationship between emotional and physical well-being in the aftermath of pet loss, we can create spaces of empathy, understanding, and healing for those navigating the often underestimated depths of grief.

Research in the Field of Pet Loss

Research on the grief process related to losing a pet has become an increasingly recognized field within psychology, veterinary medicine, and sociology. The exploration of the emotional impact of pet loss has shed light on the complexity and depth of the human-animal bond.

Psychological Impact

Numerous studies have explored the psychological impact of pet loss, emphasizing that the grief experienced can be as intense as that felt for the loss of a human family member. Research indicates that the emotional attachment to pets is profound and that individuals may go through similar stages of grief, including denial, anger, bargaining, depression, and acceptance.

Anticipatory Grief

Some studies delve into anticipatory grief in the context of pet loss. As pets age or face terminal illnesses, owners often experience a form of grief before the actual loss occurs. This research helps to understand the unique challenges and emotional experiences of individuals who grapple with the impending loss of a beloved pet.

Attachment Theory

Psychological theories like attachment theory have been applied to the human-pet bond. Research explores how individuals form emotional attachments to their pets, examining the impact of these attachments on the grieving process. Attachment theory helps explain the bond's depth and the loss's emotional significance.

Grief Duration and Intensity

Studies have investigated the duration and intensity of grief after pet loss. While grief is a highly individualized experience, research aims to identify common patterns and factors influencing the length and severity of grief. This knowledge aids in developing effective support strategies for individuals navigating the grieving process.

Societal Attitudes and Support

Research has explored societal attitudes toward pet loss and the availability of support. Understanding how pet loss is perceived by others and the level of support available can influence how individuals cope with grief. Additionally, studies highlight the need for increased societal recognition and support for those mourning the loss of a pet.

Physical Health Impacts

Investigations into the physical health impacts of pet loss have revealed that grief can have measurable effects on an individual's health. Changes in sleep patterns, appetite, and overall well-being have been documented. Researchers aim to identify the connections between emotional grief and physical health to guide holistic approaches to coping.

Pet Loss Support Programs

The development and evaluation of pet loss support programs have been subjects of research. Studies assess the effectiveness of counseling, support groups, and other interventions in helping individuals cope with the unique challenges of pet loss. The goal is to identify best practices for providing emotional support and facilitating healing.

Cultural and Cross-Cultural Perspectives

Cultural and cross-cultural perspectives on pet loss grief have been explored. Different cultures may have varying attitudes toward pets and diverse ways of expressing grief. Understanding these cultural nuances contributes to developing more inclusive and culturally sensitive approaches to supporting individuals through pet loss.

Children and Pet Loss

Research also examines how children experience and cope with the loss of a pet. Studies explore the role of pets in children's lives, the impact of pet loss on their emotional development, and effective strategies for supporting grieving children.

The body of research on the grief process of losing a pet is diverse and interdisciplinary. It encompasses psychological, sociological, and health-related perspectives, aiming to comprehensively understand the unique dynamics of pet loss grief and develop supportive interventions for individuals and communities.

As we conclude this exploration into the profound and intricate bond between pets and humans, it becomes evident that the connection forged between these species transcends the ordinary. Our homes are not merely shared spaces but sanctuaries of mutual understanding, companionship, and unconditional love. Whether manifested in the joyful leaps of a dog, the rhythmic purring of a cat, or the quiet presence of smaller companions, the human-animal bond creates many shared experiences and emotions.

As we turn the page into the next chapter, we embark on a journey through the intricate landscapes of grief. The bond we share with our pets while enriching our lives immeasurably also introduces us to loss's nuanced and often challenging terrain. In the upcoming pages, we will delve into the depths of grief accompanying our cherished companions' departure. We will explore the many ways in which pet loss touches the core of our emotional and physical well-being, seeking understanding, solace, and avenues for healing.

Grief, with its many facets, is a universal human experience, yet the grief over losing a pet carries its own unique complexities. The bond formed with our furry friends creates a connection that defies easy categorization, and as we navigate the landscapes of sorrow, we will unravel the layers of emotions, challenges, and healing accompanying this distinctive form of loss.

Join me as we embark on this empathetic exploration, a journey that seeks not only to comprehend the depths of pet loss grief but also to provide comfort, understanding, and practical strategies for navigating the intricate paths of sorrow. Together, we will navigate the shadows of grief, acknowledging the significance of the human-animal bond and embracing the shared experiences that unite us on this poignant journey of healing and remembrance.

CHAPTER THREE

Understanding Grief

In the tender spaces of our hearts, we embark on an exploration of grief as it intertwines with the loss of a beloved pet. This chapter invites us to navigate the emotional landscape, seeking to understand the intricate stages and nuanced types of grief accompanying the profound experience of saying goodbye to our furry companions.

The bond between humans and their pets transcends the ordinary. As we navigate the realm of pet loss, we encounter grief in its many forms—each as unique as the relationship we once shared with our animal friends. Understanding the stages and types of grief becomes a lantern, gently illuminating the path as we navigate the complex terrain of sorrow.

In the upcoming pages, we'll delve into the universal stages of grief, acknowledging their presence in the context of pet loss. From denial to acceptance, each stage leaves its imprint on our hearts, guiding us through the maze of emotions.

This chapter serves as a compass, offering insights and reflections to those grappling with the unique challenges of pet loss. As we delve into the depths of our emotions, may we discover solace, understanding, and a sense of connection with others who have walked a similar path. Together, let us begin this empathetic journey, seeking to comprehend the stages and types of grief that accompany the loss of our beloved animal companions.

The Grieving Process

The five stages of grief, as introduced by psychiatrist Elisabeth Kübler-Ross, provide a framework for understanding the emotional process individuals go through when facing significant loss. When applied to the context of losing a pet, these stages offer insights into the complex and often nuanced journey of pet loss grief.

Denial

In the context of losing a pet, denial may manifest as an initial disbelief or shock at the reality of the situation. When faced with the sudden absence of a beloved companion, individuals may find themselves momentarily unable to grasp the permanence of the loss. Denial serves as a protective mechanism, providing a buffer against the overwhelming wave of emotions that follows.

Anger

Anger, a natural response to grief, can be directed at various sources when losing a pet. Some individuals may find themselves angry at the circumstances surrounding their pet's death, at perceived injustices, or even at themselves for not being able to prevent the loss. The intensity of this anger often mirrors the depth of the bond with the pet and the profound sense of helplessness accompanying their departure.

Bargaining

The bargaining stage involves attempts to negotiate or make deals to reverse or alleviate the loss. In the context of losing a pet, individuals might engage in internal dialogues, make promises, or wish for a scenario in which their pet could be returned. Bargaining is often fueled by the desperate desire to turn back time and rewrite the narrative that led to the loss.

Depression

Depression in the grieving process doesn't solely refer to clinical depression but encompasses profound sadness and emotional weight. When losing a pet, this stage may involve a deep sense of loss, an overwhelming longing for the companionship that once filled the home, and a recognition of the void left by the absence of the pet's presence. Depression in pet loss grief often reflects the depth of the bond and the acuteness of the emotional pain.

Acceptance

Acceptance does not imply a complete recovery or the absence of sorrow; rather, it represents a gradual coming to terms with the reality of the pet's absence. Individuals may start to integrate the loss into their lives, finding ways to honor the memory of their pet and adjust to a new normal. Acceptance in pet loss grief is not a linear process but a series of small steps toward finding meaning and healing in the midst of the profound loss.

It's crucial to note that these stages are not necessarily experienced linearly, and individuals may move back and forth between them. Furthermore, the grieving process is highly individualized, influenced by factors such as the nature of the bond with the pet, the circumstances of the loss, and the individual's coping mechanisms. Recognizing the unique journey of grief in the context of losing a pet allows for a more compassionate understanding of the emotional complexities involved.

How the Stages of Grief May Manifest in Pet Owners

The stages of grief for a pet owner, while sharing similarities with the grieving process for other losses, are uniquely impacted by the distinctive nature of the human-animal bond. Several factors contribute to the differences in how pet owners experience and navigate the stages of grief.

Unconditional Love and Non-Judgmental Companionship:

Pets provide a unique form of companionship marked by unconditional love and acceptance. Unlike human relationships, the bond with a pet is free from judgment, criticism, or expectation. This depth of emotional connection amplifies the intensity of grief when a pet is lost, as the pet served as a constant source of comfort, joy, and unwavering loyalty.

Non-Verbal Communication

The communication between pets and their owners is often non-verbal but incredibly rich in emotional depth. Pet owners may mourn the loss of a physical presence and the unique ways their pet communicated and understood them. The absence of this silent but profound connection can heighten the emotional impact of the grief process.

Daily Routines and Companionship

Pets become integral parts of their owners' daily routines. Losing a pet disrupts these routines, leaving voids in morning walks, playtime, and shared quiet moments. The absence of a constant companion can make daily life feel starkly different, and adjusting to this new reality becomes an intrinsic part of the grieving process for pet owners.

Stigma and Societal Understanding

There is still a certain level of stigma or lack of societal understanding regarding the depth of grief experienced when a pet is lost. Some individuals may struggle to comprehend the intensity of the bond between a pet and their owner, which can leave grieving pet owners feeling isolated or invalidated in their grief. This societal reaction influences how pet owners navigate and express their grief.

Decision-Making and Guilt

Pet owners often face unique decisions related to their pets' care and end-of-life choices. The responsibility of making decisions about euthanasia, quality of life, and end-of-life care can introduce layers of guilt and second-guessing. While made out of love and concern for the pet's well-being, these decisions can contribute to the complexity of grief for pet owners.

Shorter Lifespan

In many cases, pets have shorter lifespans than humans. This reality means that pet owners may face the loss of multiple pets throughout their lives. The cumulative impact of these losses, coupled with the relatively brief time spent with each pet, can create a unique landscape of grief marked by repeated cycles of attachment and loss.

Anthropomorphism and Unique Bonds

Humans often anthropomorphize their pets, attributing human-like qualities, emotions, and personalities to them. This tendency deepens the sense of connection and makes the loss more akin to losing a family member. The unique bonds forged with pets, sometimes characterized by shared routines, rituals, and a shared language, contribute to the distinctiveness of pet loss grief.

The stages of grief for a pet owner are influenced by the special qualities of the human-animal bond, societal attitudes toward pet loss, and the unique challenges associated with decision-making and shorter lifespans. Recognizing these differences allows for a more compassionate understanding of the grieving process for those who have lost a beloved pet.

Normalizing Pet Loss Grief

In the tender embrace of your grief, I want you to know that every tear shed for your beloved companion is a testament to the profound love that defined your connection. In the quiet corners of your heart, where memories of playful moments and comforting cuddles reside, it is entirely normal to feel the weight of loss, for pets are not merely animals; they are cherished family members, confidants, and silent witnesses to the chapters of our lives.

In the gentle rhythm of your sorrow, understand that pet grief is not a sign of weakness but a reflection of the immeasurable bond you shared. The pain you carry echoes the love that once filled your home, the pawprints left on the landscape of your heart. It is okay to mourn, to ache for the familiar presence that graced your days with joy and warmth.

Your grief is valid, comprised of love, companionship, and shared moments that etched themselves into the fabric of your existence. The quiet sighs, the longing glances toward an empty bed, and the silent conversations with an absent friend are sacred expressions of love that transcend the boundaries between species.

In the understanding gaze of your sorrow, acknowledge that pet grief is a universal language spoken by compassionate hearts around the world. It is a language that whispers, "You are not alone," and embraces the depth of your emotions without judgment. Your grief is not a fleeting sentiment but a testament to the richness of the human-animal bond, a bond that defies easy categorization and leaves an indelible mark on the canvas of your soul.

As you navigate the labyrinth of emotions, grant yourself the grace to mourn, reminisce, and honor your cherished companion's memory.

Your grief is not a sign of fragility but a courageous acknowledgment of the profound impact your pet had on your life. In this sacred space of remembrance, know that you are seen and heard, and your grief is wholly, unequivocally, and beautifully normal.

A Woman and Her Beloved Cat

In a quaint village, there lived an elderly woman named Margaret. Her days were painted with the hues of routine, and at the heart of her quiet existence was a devoted feline companion named Whiskers.

Whiskers, a tuxedo cat with an air of regality, entered Margaret's life as a scrawny kitten found abandoned near her doorstep. An unspoken bond blossomed from that moment, transforming Margaret's routine into a series of shared moments. Whiskers became her confidant, her silent companion through the ups and downs of life, offering solace with a gentle purr and understanding eyes that seemed to peer into the depths of her soul.

As the years passed, the duo forged a unique language of their own. Whiskers knew the rhythm of Margaret's heart, the cadence of her footsteps, and the melodies of her laughter. They became inseparable, their days intertwined in routine and shared affections.

However, the inevitable passage of time brought the harsh reality of aging for Margaret and Whiskers. Once agile and spry, the feline began to move with a measured grace, and Margaret, too, felt the weight of the years settling upon her shoulders. Yet, their bond endured, resilient in the face of the changes time wrought upon them.

Then, one autumn evening, as the leaves painted the world in shades of gold, Whiskers curled up beside Margaret, his purrs a gentle lullaby. In the quiet stillness, he closed his eyes for the last time, leaving Margaret to face the deafening silence that followed. Like a sudden gust of wind, the loss swept through the corners of her home, leaving an emptiness that echoed in every room.

Margaret, once a pillar of strength, found herself navigating a sea of grief deeper than she had ever known. The familiar rituals of feeding, brushing, and the comforting weight of Whiskers on her lap vanished, leaving behind an ache that seemed insurmountable. The routine that once brought solace became a haunting reminder of what was no more.

Days turned into nights, and Margaret wandered through the labyrinth of grief, her heart heavy with the weight of absence. She planted a small garden in Whiskers' favorite spot, whispering tales of their adventures as she tended to the blossoming flowers. The void left by her feline friend seemed to echo in the quiet moments, and tears, like delicate raindrops, became a familiar companion.

In the midst of her sorrow, Margaret discovered a treasure trove of memories stored in photographs, paw prints in clay, and a worn-out toy that carried the echoes of Whiskers' playful days. She realized that grieving deeply was not a sign of weakness but a testament to the profound love they had shared.

As the seasons continued to cycle, Margaret slowly began to heal. The pain of loss did not evaporate entirely, but it transformed into a gentle ache—a reminder of the beautiful chapter of her life written in paw prints and whiskers.

In the quiet of her home, surrounded by the whispers of memories, Margaret found solace in the knowledge that the love she and Whiskers shared transcended the boundaries of time. Their story became a melody, played softly in the rustling leaves and blooming flowers, a testament to the enduring bond between a woman and her feline confidant.

Margaret's grief over losing Whiskers is not only normal but also a poignant reflection of the deep and profound bond that existed between them. The intensity of Margaret's sorrow is entirely understandable and falls within the spectrum of normal responses to pet loss. Several aspects of her grief affirm its normalcy.

Deep Emotional Connection

Margaret and Whiskers shared a bond that extended beyond mere companionship. Whiskers was Margaret's confidant, a source of comfort, and a presence that wove through the fabric of her daily life. The depth of their emotional connection created a unique relationship, and the grief Margaret experiences is a natural response to the profound love they shared.

Significant Life Presence

Whiskers was not just a pet; he played a significant role in Margaret's life. His daily routines, purring companionship, and the unspoken language they developed over the years became integral to Margaret's sense of well-being. The absence of such a meaningful presence inevitably leads to a deep sense of loss and grief.

Shared History and Memories

Margaret and Whiskers created a tapestry of shared memories. Their journey together, from Whiskers' kittenhood to his graceful aging, formed an intricate part of Margaret's life story. The richness of their shared history contributes to the depth of Margaret's grief, as each memory carries the weight of their unique bond.

Rituals of Remembrance

Margaret's actions reflect healthy and adaptive coping mechanisms, such as planting a garden in Whiskers' favorite spot and tending to it with whispered tales of their adventures. These rituals of remembrance are common in grief, providing individuals with a tangible way to honor their lost companions and maintain a connection with them.

Acknowledgment of Grief

Margaret's tears are not signs of weakness but expressions of her love for Whiskers. The acknowledgment of her grief, the willingness to feel and express the pain of loss, is a crucial aspect of the grieving process. It reflects a healthy emotional response to Whiskers' profound impact on Margaret's life.

Healing Through Memories

Margaret's slow healing process, marked by the discovery of a treasure trove of memories, signifies a healthy approach to grief. While the pain may not completely dissipate, Margaret learns to carry the memories of Whiskers with her as a source of solace and a reminder of the enduring love they shared.

Margaret's grief over losing Whiskers is entirely normal and reflective of her extraordinary connection with her feline companion. Grieving deeply for a pet is a testament to the significance of the human-animal bond and our furry friends' enduring impact on the fabric of our lives. Margaret's journey through grief is a poignant reminder that the love we share with our pets leaves an indelible mark, and grieving their loss is a natural and necessary part of the healing process.

Complicated Grief

Complicated grief, also known as prolonged grief disorder, is a form of grief that extends beyond the typical duration and intensity associated with the mourning process. Grief becomes complicated when the bereaved individual struggles to adapt to the loss, experiencing persistent and debilitating symptoms that impede their ability to resume a normal life. This condition can make it challenging for individuals to find closure and move forward.

Factors Contributing to Complicated Grief

Several factors can contribute to transforming grief into complicated grief. It's important to note that each experience is unique to the individual and not everyone will experience complications.

Lack of Social Support

Limited or insufficient support from family and friends can contribute to the complexity of grief. Feeling isolated in the grieving process may exacerbate emotional distress. Self-isolation can also lead to a lack of social support.

Sudden or Traumatic Loss

Complicated grief is more likely to occur when the loss is sudden, unexpected, or accompanied by trauma. Such circumstances can make it difficult for individuals to process their emotions and come to terms with the reality of the loss.

Pre-existing Mental Health Conditions

Individuals with pre-existing mental health conditions, such as depression or anxiety, may be more susceptible to complicated grief. These conditions can amplify the emotional impact of loss and hinder the ability to cope.

Complicated Relationship with the Deceased

The nature of the relationship with the deceased can influence the grieving process. Complicated grief may occur when the relationship was marked by unresolved conflicts, ambivalence, or an unhealthy dependency.

Multiple Losses

Experiencing multiple losses within a short timeframe can overwhelm an individual's ability to cope, leading to complicated grief. Each subsequent loss may compound the grief associated with previous losses.

Signs of Complicated Grief

While complicated grief is not an everyday occurrence, it is important to understand the signs. It can be challenging to manage on your own. If you or someone else has any of these signs following the loss of a pet, it's likely you are experiencing complicated grief and may need to seek professional help to guide you through the rocky landscape of grief.

Intense Longing and Preoccupation

Individuals with complicated grief may exhibit persistent longing and preoccupation with the deceased. Thoughts and memories of the lost loved one dominate their daily life, making it challenging to focus on other aspects of living.

Inability to Accept the Loss

A key feature of complicated grief is difficulty accepting the reality of the loss. The bereaved person may engage in behaviors that maintain a sense of connection with the deceased, such as avoiding the possessions of the deceased or refusing to discuss the loss.

Emotional Numbness or Detachment

Some individuals may experience emotional numbness or detachment as a way to cope with the pain. They may withdraw from social interactions, struggle to experience positive emotions, and exhibit a pervasive sense of emptiness.

Functional Impairment

Complicated grief can significantly impair an individual's ability to carry out daily activities, maintain relationships, or fulfill work responsibilities. The persistent impact on daily functioning is a notable sign that grief has become complicated.

Persistent Grief Symptoms

While grief symptoms naturally fluctuate over time, in complicated grief, they persist or even intensify beyond the typical mourning period. Symptoms may include sadness, guilt, anger, and a sense of meaninglessness.

When to Seek Professional Help

It is essential to seek professional help if you observe signs of complicated grief or if the grieving process significantly interferes with daily life. Consider seeking help if:

- **Symptoms Persist**: Grief symptoms persist for an extended period, typically beyond six months, without any signs of improvement.

- **Functional Impairment**: The grief-related distress significantly impairs the ability to perform daily tasks, maintain relationships, or fulfill work obligations.

- **Intense Emotional Pain**: Intense emotional pain, including feelings of hopelessness, persists, and the grieving individual is unable to find relief.

- **Isolation and Withdrawal**: The bereaved person withdraws from social interactions, experiencing isolation and an inability to connect with others.

- **Thoughts of Self-Harm**: Any thoughts of self-harm or suicidal ideation require immediate professional intervention.

Professional help may involve therapy, counseling, or support groups specializing in grief and loss. Mental health professionals can provide guidance, support, and coping strategies tailored to the unique challenges of complicated grief. It is crucial to prioritize one's mental health and seek assistance when needed, as timely intervention can significantly improve the trajectory of the healing process.

In the ebb and flow of grief, we have embarked on a journey to unravel its intricacies, exploring the depths of sorrow, the varied manifestations of mourning, and the factors that can complicate the healing process. Understanding grief is not just an academic pursuit but a compassionate exploration of the human experience when faced with loss. As we conclude this chapter, it's essential to acknowledge that grief is a highly individual journey—personal, profound, and deeply human.

In the gentle whispers of memories and the echoes of shared stories, we find solace in recognizing that grief is a testament to the love we hold for those who have touched our lives. Each tear shed and every heartache are a tribute to the bonds we forged and our beloved pets' impact on our existence.

As we turn the page to the next chapter, we delve into a different facet of the human-animal bond—one marked by difficult decisions, compassion, and the unspoken act of letting go. In understanding when it's time to bid farewell to our cherished companions, we navigate a terrain where love and responsibility intersect, and the profound lessons of companionship take on a new form.

Join me in this exploration, where we seek to comprehend the complexities of making decisions about our pets' well-being. We tread carefully, guided by the love that binds us to our furry friends, and we learn to navigate the delicate balance between holding on and letting go. As we embark on this next chapter, may it offer insights, comfort, and a compassionate guide for those facing the challenging crossroads of pet ownership and the deeply emotional process of saying goodbye.

Chapter Four

When It's Time to Say Goodbye

During our shared journey with our beloved pets, there comes a time when our roles as caregivers take on a profound responsibility—an act of love that is both heart-wrenching and compassionate. In this chapter, we delicately approach the poignant subject of bidding farewell to our cherished companions.

Our furry friends, with their unwavering loyalty and unspoken understanding, become beloved members of our families. As devoted guardians, we are entrusted with the well-being of these gentle souls, and therein lies the weight of a decision that transcends the ordinary rhythms of pet ownership. Recognizing when it's time to say goodbye is an act of love, a testament to our bond, and a compassionate acknowledgment of our pets' dignity and comfort.

In the following pages, we navigate the emotions, the uncertainties, and the delicate balance between holding on and letting go. It is a journey marked by compassion, filled with moments of reflection, and guided by the deep love that has defined our connection with our pets.

This chapter aims to provide a supportive guide for those facing the difficult decision of saying farewell to their furry companions. As we explore the considerations, emotions, and compassionate choices involved, may these words serve as a source of understanding, comfort, and solace for hearts weighed down by the tender responsibility of deciding when to say goodbye. Together, let us navigate this emotional landscape with compassion, grace, and an enduring love that transcends the boundaries between us and our cherished pets.

Anticipating the Loss

In the twilight moments of our pets' lives, as caregivers, we are faced with profound decisions that blend love and responsibility. Providing end-of-life care for a beloved pet is a challenging path marked by compassion, difficult choices, and an unwavering commitment to their well-being.

Understanding the Quality of Life:

Begin by attuning yourself to your pet's quality of life. Observe their behavior, appetite, and overall demeanor. Are they still finding joy in activities, or do they seem fatigued and disinterested? Assess their pain level and any signs of distress. Your keen observations will serve as gentle guides in understanding their comfort and happiness.

Consulting with Veterinarians

Engage in open and honest conversations with your veterinarian. They are not only medical experts but compassionate allies on this journey. Discuss your pet's condition, prognosis, and potential treatment options. Seek their guidance on pain management and the overall well-being of your pet. A collaborative approach between you and your veterinarian ensures a well-informed decision-making process.

Exploring Treatment Options

If medical interventions are available, consider the potential benefits and drawbacks. Understand the treatment's impact on your pet's comfort, their ability to engage in normal activities, and the potential side effects. Balance the benefits with the potential stress or discomfort associated with the treatment. This delicate equilibrium will help guide your decision.

Ensuring Comfort and Dignity

Prioritize your pet's comfort and dignity above all else. Create a serene and comforting environment for them. Provide soft bedding, soothing music, or familiar scents. As you make decisions about their care, envision a setting that reflects the love and respect you've shared throughout their life.

Incorporating Palliative Care

Consider the role of palliative care to enhance your pet's quality of life. Palliative care focuses on managing pain and providing comfort, allowing your pet to experience a sense of peace and tranquility. This approach can be a valuable component of end-of-life care, ensuring your pet's final days are filled with love and comfort.

Deciding on Euthanasia

The decision to euthanize a pet is undeniably one of the most challenging aspects of end-of-life care. Approach this decision with deep empathy and a profound understanding of your pet's condition. Reflect on their quality of life and consider whether their suffering has become unmanageable. When the time comes, be present with your pet, offering reassurance, love, and comfort.

Creating Lasting Memories

As you navigate these difficult decisions, cherish the moments you have left with your pet. Create a scrapbook of memories, capturing the essence of their unique personality. Take photographs, share stories, and engage in activities that bring joy. These precious moments become a testament to the love you've shared, forming a comforting tapestry of memories.

In this challenging journey of end-of-life care, remember that you are not alone. Seek support from friends, family, or support groups who understand the depth of your bond with your pet. Let compassion be your guiding light, and may your decisions be infused with love, understanding, and the unwavering commitment to ensuring your pet's well-being until their final moments.

Preparing for the Final Goodbye

In the tender moments leading up to a cherished pet's expected loss, it's natural to feel a cascade of emotions—anticipation, grief, and a profound sense of love. Preparing emotionally and mentally for this inevitable transition is a journey that requires patience, self-compassion, and an acknowledgment of the unique bond you share with your furry friend.

Acknowledge Your Feelings

First and foremost, grant yourself the grace to acknowledge and express your emotions. Whether it's sadness, anxiety, or a mix of various feelings, understand that each sentiment is a testament to the deep connection you have with your pet. Allow these emotions to surface, for they are an integral part of the healing process.

Create Meaningful Moments

Take intentional moments to create lasting memories with your pet. Engage in activities that bring joy to both of you—whether it's a gentle stroll in the park, a cozy afternoon snuggle, or a favorite treat. These shared moments become treasures that can bring comfort in the days to come.

Open Communication

Share your feelings with those around you, especially with family and friends who understand the unique relationship you have with your pet. Sometimes, verbalizing your emotions can provide a sense of relief and foster an environment of support. Share stories, reminisce about happy times, and allow the love you feel for your pet to be celebrated.

Quality Time

Spend quality time with your pet, engaging in activities that bring them comfort and joy. This intentional time allows you to deepen your bond and assures your pet that they are cherished until the very end. Whether it's a gentle stroke, a whispered word, or simply being present, your companionship is a source of solace for both you and your pet.

Create a Comforting Environment

As the expected loss approaches, focus on creating a calm and comforting environment for your pet. Ensure they have a favorite spot, soft bedding, and familiar scents. This atmosphere of familiarity can alleviate stress for your pet and offer them a sense of security.

Connect with Supportive Resources

Seek out supportive resources such as pet loss support groups, online forums, or counseling services. Sharing your feelings with those who have experienced similar journeys can provide valuable insights, comfort, and a sense of community during this challenging time.

Express Gratitude

Take moments to express gratitude for the love and companionship your pet has brought into your life. Reflect on their positive impact on your well-being and the countless memories that have enriched your days. Expressing gratitude can be a therapeutic way to honor the bond you've shared.

Self-Care

Amidst the emotional preparations, prioritize self-care. Take moments to engage in activities that comfort you—reading, spending time in nature, or enjoying a quiet cup of tea. Nourish your emotional well-being, recognizing that caring for yourself is integral to caring for your pet during this tender time.

Remember, the journey of preparing emotionally for the expected loss of a pet is a testament to the love and compassion that defines the human-animal bond. Embrace these moments with tenderness, knowing that the love you share with your pet is enduring and that your thoughtful preparations reflect the depth of that love.

The Euthanasia Decision

Deciding on euthanasia for a beloved pet is undeniably one of the most heart-wrenching and compassionate decisions a pet owner may face. It's a choice imbued with love, empathy, and a profound commitment to ensuring your furry friend's well-being, even in their final moments. Here is some guidance to navigate this difficult decision with compassion.

Begin by conducting a thoughtful and honest assessment of your pet's quality of life. Consider their ability to engage in normal activities, experience joy, and manage pain. Look for signs of distress, discomfort, or a diminishing interest in things that once brought them happiness. This assessment serves as a foundation for understanding your pet's current well-being.

Engage in open and transparent communication with your veterinarian. They are medical professionals and empathetic guides who can provide valuable insights into your pet's condition, prognosis, and potential treatment options. Collaborate with your veterinarian to understand the available choices, the impact of those choices on your pet's comfort, and the potential outcomes.

If treatment options are available, carefully weigh the benefits and drawbacks. Consider the potential impact on your pet's overall well-being, their ability to engage in normal activities, and the potential side effects. It's crucial to find a balance between extending their quality of life and avoiding unnecessary stress or discomfort.

The decision to euthanize is about timing as much as it is about love. Reflect on whether your pet can still enjoy moments of happiness, receive love, and maintain their dignity. While it's a difficult decision, choosing euthanasia at the right time ensures that your pet is spared unnecessary suffering.

While they may not understand the words, your pet is attuned to your emotions and presence. Spend quiet, comforting moments with them, expressing your love and gratitude. This connection can be a source of reassurance for both you and your pet.

Recognize the impact of your pet's condition on your own emotional well-being. If witnessing their suffering becomes emotionally overwhelming, it's a valid consideration in the decision-making process. Your ability to provide comfort and support is an essential aspect of their final moments.

Share your feelings with family and friends who understand the depth of your bond with your pet. Their support and empathy can be invaluable during this emotionally challenging time. Sometimes, verbalizing your emotions provides relief and fosters an environment of understanding.

When the time comes, ensure your pet's environment is calm and comforting. Familiar scents, soft bedding, and your reassuring presence can provide a sense of security and ease any anxiety they may feel.

Acknowledge that while the decision to euthanize is an act of love, it is also one that brings profound grief. Allow yourself the time and space to grieve, understanding that it is a natural part of the healing process. Seek support from those who understand the unique bond you shared with your pet.

For the Love of Luna

In the quiet corners of his home, where sunlight spilled through the windows and the familiar scent of comfort lingered, Peter found himself facing the agonizing crossroads that every pet owner dreads—the decision to say a tearful goodbye through the merciful act of euthanasia.

Her name was Luna, a gentle soul wrapped in fur who had been Peter's loyal companion for over a decade. They had shared countless sunsets, weathered life's storms, and carved memories that adorned the walls of their shared existence. Luna, with her soulful eyes and a heart that beat in sync with Peter's, had become an integral part of the very fabric of his life.

As the years advanced, Luna's once vibrant steps became hesitant, her playful barks replaced by soft whimpers. Time, that silent artist, had painted its inevitable strokes on her once-lustrous coat. Arthritis had claimed the agility that defined her, and a quiet pain lingered in her eyes—a language only Peter could decipher.

The decision to consider euthanasia began as a whisper, a hesitant acknowledgment that the sands of time were running out for his dear friend. Peter sought guidance from a compassionate veterinarian who witnessed Luna's journey from frolicking puppyhood to the gentle twilight of her golden years. With empathy etched across her face, the vet spoke of Luna's diminishing quality of life, the pain that lingered beneath the surface, and the limited options for relief.

Each day became a delicate dance between love and the impending grief that loomed on the horizon. Luna, ever attuned to Peter's emotions, met his gaze with trust and an unspoken understanding. Their daily rituals became imbued with a bittersweet awareness—a final stroll in the garden, shared moments of stillness, and the soft murmur of whispered conversations.

The day arrived, heavy with the weight of sorrow. Nestled in her favorite spot, Luna looked at Peter with eyes that mirrored a lifetime of shared secrets and unwavering trust. The vet, a gentle presence, explained the process with kindness and reassurance. Peter held Luna close, feeling the rise and fall of her breath, committing the warmth of her fur and the rhythm of her heartbeat to memory.

As the final moments unfolded, a cascade of emotions enveloped Peter—a mixture of heartache and an overwhelming sense of love. With a soft exhale, Luna surrendered to the peace that awaited her. Once filled with the echoes of their shared existence, the room became a sanctuary of quietude.

In the days that followed, grief poured forth in waves—tears that held the weight of a thousand shared moments. Yet, within that grief, there lingered a profound gratitude. Gratitude for the gift of Luna's companionship, for the love that had bound them together, and for the mercy that allowed her to depart with dignity.

Choosing euthanasia for Luna was a testament to the depth of their connection—a final act of love that transcended the pain of separation. In the quiet spaces of his home, where Luna's presence still whispered through the walls, Peter carried forward the enduring love that defined their journey. And in the echoes of their shared moments, Luna's spirit lingered—a gentle reminder that love, even in its most painful form, endures beyond the boundaries of time.

Natural Death

Coping with a pet's natural death is a deeply emotional journey, one that requires patience, self-compassion, and an acknowledgment of the unique bond you shared with your beloved companion. The nuances of this process extend from the initial moments of realization to the ongoing journey of healing after your pet has crossed the rainbow bridge.

How to Navigate a Natural Death

The first step in coping with a pet's natural death is acknowledging your grief. Allow yourself to feel the profound sadness, recognizing that the depth of your emotions attests. to the love and connection you shared with your pet. Grieving is a natural and necessary part of the healing process.

If circumstances allow, consider creating a meaningful goodbye ritual. Spend quiet moments with your pet, expressing your love and gratitude. This could involve gentle strokes, whispered words, or simply being present with them. Creating a peaceful and loving environment during their final moments can offer comfort to both you and your pet.

Grieving is a unique and personal experience, but it doesn't have to be faced alone. Seek support from friends, family, or support groups that understand the depth of the human-animal bond. Sharing your feelings and memories with others who have gone through similar experiences can provide validation and comfort.

Consider memorializing your pet in a way that holds special meaning for you. This could involve creating a scrapbook, planting a tree in their memory, or donating to a pet charity in their name. Finding a tangible way to honor your pet's legacy can be a therapeutic part of grieving.

Healing from the loss of a pet takes time, and the process is unique for everyone. Be patient with yourself and allow the emotions to ebb and flow. Understand that healing doesn't mean forgetting; rather, it involves finding a way to carry the love and memories of your pet with you as you move forward.

Seek to preserve the memories you shared with your pet. Collect photographs, write down anecdotes, or create a dedicated space in your home that serves as a loving tribute. These tangible reminders can provide solace and keep the spirit of your pet alive in your heart.

Remember, grief doesn't follow a linear path; it comes in waves. Some days may be more challenging than others, and that's okay. Allow yourself to feel the emotions as they come without judgment. Each wave of grief is a step toward healing.

If you find solace in sharing your experiences with others who are grieving the loss of a pet, consider joining a pet loss support group. These groups provide a safe space to express your feelings, gain insights from others, and find understanding in a community of individuals going through similar challenges.

As time progresses, find ways to integrate the loss into your life. This doesn't mean forgetting your pet but rather incorporating their memory into your daily routine in a comforting way. It could involve displaying a photo, creating a memorial, or finding other meaningful ways to keep their spirit alive.

Coping with a pet's natural death is a tender and personal journey. By honoring your emotions, seeking support, and preserving the beautiful memories you shared, you can navigate this process with grace and compassion, allowing the love you and your pet shared to endure in your heart.

Feelings That May Arise

The natural death of a pet is a profoundly emotional experience, and a myriad of feelings can arise during this tender and challenging time. Each person's response is unique, influenced by the nature of the human-animal bond, the circumstances of the pet's passing, and individual coping mechanisms. Many diverse feelings may surface.

The most common and immediate emotion is grief. The deep sorrow and sadness that accompany the loss of a beloved pet are often overwhelming. It's a natural response to the absence of a cherished companion.

In cases where a pet has been suffering due to illness or age-related issues, there might be a sense of relief that their pain and discomfort have come to an end. This feeling coexists with grief and is an acknowledgment of the desire to spare the pet unnecessary suffering.

Pet owners may experience guilt, questioning if they could have done more or made different decisions regarding their pet's care. This feeling is common but important to recognize as part of the grieving process.

Additionally, the sense of loss can sometimes manifest as anger or frustration. This can be directed towards oneself, others involved in the pet's care, or even at the circumstances surrounding the pet's death.

Fond memories and nostalgia for the times shared with the pet often emerge. This can bring both comfort and a renewed sense of loss as the reality of the pet's absence settles in.

The void left by a pet's passing can lead to feelings of loneliness and emptiness. The absence of their companionship, routines, and the unique energy they brought to the household can be profoundly felt.

Regret may surface, particularly if there were missed opportunities to spend more time with the pet or if there are lingering unresolved issues. It's crucial to acknowledge regret as part of the grieving process and focus on the relationship's positive aspects.

Over time, there may be moments of acceptance, where the reality of the pet's passing is recognized, and the emotional intensity begins to subside. Acceptance is a gradual process and varies from person to person.

Amidst the sorrow, there is often a profound sense of love and gratitude for the positive impact the pet had on the owner's life. Cherished memories, shared experiences, and the unique bond formed can become a source of comfort.

Facing life without the constant presence of a pet can evoke anxiety about the future. Adjusting to a new routine, redefining the home environment, and navigating daily life without their familiar companionship can be challenging.

It's important to recognize that these feelings are fluid, and individuals may move through them at their own pace. The grieving process is a unique journey, and acknowledging and expressing these emotions, whether through self-reflection, talking with others, or seeking professional support, is crucial for healing.

Providing Peace and Comfort

Providing comfort to a dying pet is an act of profound compassion and requires an intuitive understanding of their needs. It involves creating an environment of love, tranquility, and reassurance as they navigate the final moments of their journey.

Your presence is a source of immense comfort to a dying pet. Spend time near them, offering gentle strokes, soft words, and simply being there. Your familiar presence can alleviate anxiety and provide a sense of security.

Use gentle touches to convey love and comfort. Soft strokes along their fur or a soothing massage can provide physical and emotional relief. Pay attention to their cues, and adjust your touch based on their preferences.

Additionally, keep the environment familiar. Surround them with their favorite blanket, toys, or bedding. Familiar scents can provide a sense of comfort and ease any distress. Play soft, calming music or create a quiet atmosphere. Soothing sounds can calm both pets and humans, fostering a peaceful environment during their final moments.

Speak to your pet in a calm and reassuring tone. Even if they can't respond in the usual way, your voice can be a source of familiarity and comfort. Share comforting words and express your love.

Be attentive to your pet's preferences. If they seek solitude, provide a quiet space. If they prefer close contact, stay nearby. Understanding their needs in these final moments is an act of profound care.

If appropriate, consider palliative care measures to manage any pain or discomfort. Consult with your veterinarian to explore options that prioritize your pet's well-being and provide them with the most comfort possible.

Engage in activities your pet loves, tailored to their current abilities. Whether it's a favorite treat, a gentle game, or simply enjoying time in the sun, these activities can bring moments of joy and connection. However, you must also be mindful of their physical capabilities and comfort when choosing physical activity.

Maintain a calm and composed demeanor. Pets are highly attuned to their owners' emotions. Your peaceful presence can have a soothing effect on them as they navigate this transition. Shower them with love. Your unconditional love is a comforting and reassuring force. Let them feel the warmth of your affection, creating an environment filled with love and understanding.

In these delicate moments, the essence of providing comfort lies in your genuine connection with your pet. Pay attention to their cues, respond with love, and create an environment that reflects the deep bond you share. Your presence and care offer solace and companionship as your pet approaches the end of their journey.

As we navigate the heart-wrenching decision of when it's time to say goodbye to our cherished companions, we find ourselves standing at the precipice of a profound transition. In the delicate balance between love and letting go, we honor the sacred duty of ensuring our pets find peace, comfort, and dignity in their final moments. The decision to say farewell is a testament to the depth of our love, a poignant acknowledgment of the interconnectedness that binds us to our furry friends.

As we turn the pages of our journey, the poignant moment of loss looms on the horizon. The air is thick with emotions, and our hearts bear the weight of both sorrow and gratitude for the beautiful moments we've shared. The upcoming chapter delves into navigating the immediate aftermath of a pet's passing. The tender emotions, the quiet echoes of their absence, and the gentle process of honoring their memory become the focus as we traverse the realms of grief.

The next chapter invites us to embrace the inevitable waves of sorrow, finding solace in the memories that continue to paint our hearts with the brushstrokes of love. In the delicate movement between saying goodbye and facing the reality of loss, we discover the strength to navigate this tender terrain. Together, let us tread softly forward, where the profundity of pet loss unfolds and the journey toward healing and understanding continues.

Chapter Five
The Moment of Loss

In the bond we form with our pets, we find a love that transcends the ordinary, a connection that weaves itself into the fabric of our daily lives. Yet, in the natural course of our journey together, a moment arrives that carries the weight of profound sorrow—the moment of saying goodbye. This chapter delves into the intricacies of that juncture when we bid farewell to our cherished companions.

As we navigate the delicate terrain of parting ways with our pets, we are confronted with a spectrum of emotions—grief, gratitude, and the profound acknowledgment of the bond that has defined our shared existence. Saying goodbye is a nuanced act that demands both courage and tenderness, a moment where love and loss intertwine in a dance of farewell.

In the following pages, we explore the dynamics of this bittersweet moment, capturing the essence of saying goodbye to a beloved pet. From the gentle touch of a final caress to the whispered words of gratitude, we unravel the layers of emotion accompanying this inevitable parting. Join me as we navigate the intricate tapestry of farewells, finding solace in the love that persists even as we utter the tender words, "Goodbye, dear friend."

The Final Farewell

Creating meaningful farewell rituals for a beloved pet is a poignant and deeply personal endeavor. These rituals can offer solace, honor the unique bond shared, and provide a tangible way to express love and gratitude.

As you stand on the threshold of saying goodbye to your cherished companion, consider weaving their departure with meaningful farewell rituals—gentle acts of love that honor the depth of your bond.

The Final Stroll

Consider taking your pet for a final stroll in a place they love in these precious moments. Whether it's a favorite park, a quiet trail, or the familiar corners of your backyard, let them soak in the scents, feel the breeze, and revel in the surroundings they have known and cherished. This gentle walk becomes a pilgrimage, a reflective journey marking the conclusion of their earthly adventures.

Time for Shared Moments

Create a quiet space for shared moments. Gather your family or close friends and spend unhurried time together with your pet. Share stories, reminisce about happy times, and express your deepest gratitude for the joy and companionship your pet has brought into your lives. These shared moments become the building blocks of a farewell steeped in love and connection.

Capture Memories

Embrace the act of capturing memories. Take photographs or create a short video montage that encapsulates the essence of your pet's personality and the moments you've shared. These visual memories become tangible keepsakes, providing comfort and a visual testament to the beauty of your pet's life.

Handwritten Letters

Consider writing a heartfelt letter to your pet. Pour your emotions onto paper, expressing your love, gratitude, and the profound impact they've had on your life. This intimate act of writing becomes a cathartic release, a timeless memento that encapsulates the depth of your connection.

Paw Print Keepsake

Create a lasting imprint of your pet's paw. Use non-toxic, pet-safe ink or clay to capture their unique print. This tangible keepsake becomes a cherished reminder of the physical presence your pet once held and a symbol of the enduring imprint they leave on your heart.

Planting Seeds of Remembrance

Planting a tree, flowers, or a shrub in memory of your pet is a beautiful way to create a living tribute. As the plant grows, it symbolizes renewal and the eternal cycle of life. This living memorial serves as a poignant reminder of your enduring love and connection.

Candlelight Vigil

Organize a candlelight vigil in your pet's honor. Invite friends and family to gather in a quiet, comfortable space and light candles to create a serene atmosphere. Share stories, reflect on the beauty of your pet's spirit, and allow the gentle glow of the candles to symbolize the enduring light of their presence in your hearts.

Release of Biodegradable Balloons or Lanterns

Consider a symbolic release of biodegradable balloons or lanterns. As they ascend into the sky, carrying with them messages of love and remembrance, it becomes a poignant ritual of letting go and allowing the spirit of your pet to soar freely.

Memorialize Their Space

Dedicate a corner of your home or garden to your pet. Create a small memorial space adorned with their favorite toys, a framed photograph, and perhaps a heartfelt poem or quote. This designated area becomes a sanctuary where you can retreat to reflect on the enduring love you share.

Act of Donation

In the spirit of giving back, consider donating to a pet charity or animal welfare organization in your pet's name. This act of kindness becomes a meaningful way to honor their memory and contribute to the well-being of other animals in need.

As you engage in these heartfelt rituals, remember there is no right or wrong way to bid farewell. The essence lies in the sincerity of your actions and the profound love that fills every gesture. These rituals create part of your pet's legacy, creating an essence of remembrance that unfolds with each passing day. In these acts of love and farewell, you find solace, connection, and the enduring beauty of a bond that transcends the boundaries of time.

Stories of Goodbye Rituals

Goodbye rituals for pets are as varied as the unique relationships individuals share with their furry companions. Here are a few heartfelt examples, each offering a testament to the love and creativity that permeate the farewell process.

The Final Day Out

The Smith family made their dog's last day truly special. They took him to his favorite places, including the park for a round of fetch and the beach for a splash in the water. Joy, laughter, and shared moments filled the day, creating lasting memories of their beloved pet's favorite activities.

Paw Print Memorial

Grieving cat owner Emily created a tangible reminder of her feline friend. She carefully pressed her cat's paw onto paper using non-toxic ink, creating a paw print memorial. This simple yet heartfelt keepsake now hangs in a special corner of Emily's home, serving as a touchstone for fond memories.

Candlelit Vigil

A group of friends organized a candlelit vigil to honor their friend Sarah's departed dog. They gathered in Sarah's backyard, each holding a candle, and shared stories about the playful antics and unique quirks that made the dog special. The soft glow of candles symbolized the enduring light their furry friend brought into their lives.

Memorial Garden Planting

The Thompson family created a memorial garden in their backyard to honor their late Labrador. They planted flowers, shrubs, and a small tree in a designated area, each representing a cherished memory or characteristic of their beloved pet. The garden became a serene space for reflection and remembrance.

Commemorative Artwork

Artist Lisa expressed her grief through creativity by painting a portrait of her departed cat. The artwork captured the essence of her cat's personality and the love they shared. The painting now hangs prominently in Lisa's home, serving as a beautiful and personalized tribute.

6. Beachside Farewell

A dog who loved the beach was given a beachside farewell. The Johnson family organized a small gathering of close friends and took their dog to the shore for a final romp in the sand. They wrote messages to their furry friend on biodegradable balloons, releasing them into the sky as a symbolic farewell gesture.

Donations in Their Name

In honor of their cat's memory, the Peterson family regularly donated to a local animal shelter. Each month, they contributed supplies and funds to help other cats in need. This ongoing act of kindness became a meaningful way to pay tribute to the love their own feline friend had brought into their lives.

Shared Meal and Reminiscence

The Anderson family chose to have a simple but meaningful farewell meal together with their departed pet's favorite treats. They shared stories, laughed, and even shed tears as they reminisced about the joyful moments they had experienced with their furry companion. The act of breaking bread together became a heartfelt acknowledgment of the bond they shared.

These personalized rituals highlight the diverse and deeply personal ways in which individuals express their love and bid farewell to their beloved pets. Each ritual is a unique reflection of the special connection shared, and these acts of remembrance continue to bring solace and comfort to those navigating the journey of pet loss.

Dealing With the Immediate Aftermath

In the immediate aftermath of a pet's death, emotions can be over-whelming, and it's important to navigate this sensitive time with care and consideration. Take the time to care for yourself, honor your pet, and heal.

Take a moment to process the reality of your pet's passing. Grief is a natural and necessary response, and allowing yourself the time to mourn is crucial for healing. You can take the time to just sit with your grief. You don't need to jump up and do anything. Allow yourself to feel what you need to feel in the moment.

If your pet's death occurs at home, contact your veterinarian. They can provide guidance on what to do next, including whether to bring your pet to the clinic for further arrangements. If your pet passes away at the veterinary clinic, make sure to obtain any important documents, such as a certificate of passing or information on aftercare options.

Consider your preferences for aftercare. Options include burial, cremation, or communal cremation (where ashes are not returned). If you're unsure, your veterinarian can provide information on local services. In some areas, regulations are in place regarding what to do with the remains.

If you choose to bury your pet at home, do so with care and in compliance with local regulations. Ensure that the grave is deep enough to deter scavengers and that you use a biodegradable casket or wrap your pet in a biodegradable shroud.

When opting for cremation, contact a reputable pet crematorium. They can guide you through the process, discuss available options, and provide information on when you can expect to receive your pet's ashes if desired.

Consider creating a small memorial for your pet. This could involve placing a marker at a burial site or setting up a memorial space at home with a framed photo, a favorite toy, or other cherished mementos.

If your pet's passing affects others in your household, gently share the news and support each other. Notify close friends and family members who were part of your pet's life. Sharing the weight of the loss can help ease the pain of the experience.

Additionally, you'll also need to attend to practical matters, such as canceling or adjusting any upcoming veterinary appointments, updating records, and notifying pet-related service providers. Of course, you don't need to do this directly after the passing. You can allow yourself a few days to adjust to the situation. These are things you'll need to remember in the days following your loss.

Grieving the loss of a pet is a significant emotional experience. Reach out to friends, family, or support groups who understand the depth of the human-animal bond. Sharing your feelings can be therapeutic. If the grief becomes overwhelming, consider seeking the support of a therapist or counselor who specializes in pet loss. Professional help can provide guidance during this challenging time.

Preserving memories of your pet is beneficial for many reasons. It can help you heal from the hurt and keep them at the forefront of your thoughts. This process could involve creating a scrapbook, framing a favorite photo, or creating a digital album. These tangible reminders can bring comfort in the days and months ahead.

Taking these practical steps can help guide you through the immediate aftermath of your pet's death. Remember that grieving is a personal journey, and allowing yourself the time and space to mourn is a vital part of the healing process.

Practicing Self-Care Following the Loss of a Pet

Navigating the initial period of intense grief after the loss of a beloved pet can be emotionally challenging. It's essential to prioritize self-care during this time to support your well-being.

One of the most essential aspects of self-care is giving yourself permission to feel and express your grief. It's a natural and important part of the healing process. Allow the waves of sadness, anger, and other emotions to flow without judgment.

Don't be afraid to reach out to friends, family, or support groups who understand the unique bond between humans and their pets. Sharing your feelings with those who empathize can provide comfort and a sense of connection. Similarly, surround yourself with a supportive environment. This may involve spending time in spaces that bring you comfort, whether it's your home, a favorite park, or a quiet spot in nature.

Always be gentle with yourself. Understand that grieving takes time, and there is no right or wrong way to experience it. Treat yourself with the same kindness and understanding you would offer to a friend going through a difficult time.

Maintaining a routine can provide a sense of stability and normalcy during a time of upheaval. Establish daily rituals or activities that bring comfort, such as a morning walk or a quiet moment of reflection. While it may be difficult at first to maintain any sort of routine, getting back into the swing of things will ultimately help you get back on your feet.

Incorporating mindfulness techniques into your daily routine can help you be more centered. Whether it's meditation, deep breathing exercises, or simply being present in the moment, mindfulness can help soothe a grieving mind. The process can give you insight into the temporary state of your pain and sadness. While you will always remember and love your pet, eventually, you will heal from losing them.

Take the time to preserve memories of your pet in a way that feels meaningful to you. Create a scrapbook, compile a photo album, or write down your favorite memories. These tangible reminders can become a source of comfort.

Engaging in creative activities to express your emotions will help you release them constructively. Whether it's writing in a journal, painting, or crafting, creative outlets can provide a healthy way to process and externalize your feelings. By not keeping them tightly balled up inside, you can ease your hurt in many different ways.

Don't forget to give yourself permission to take breaks from the intensity of grief. It's okay to find moments of respite in activities that bring joy, even if briefly. If you laugh and find joy in activities, it's completely normal. Grief doesn't have to be a solid period of nothing but sadness. You are not dishonoring your pet by having a moment of happiness.

You should always pay attention to your physical health. Ensure you eat nourishing meals, stay hydrated, and get adequate rest. Physical well-being is interconnected with emotional well-being. While grief takes a significant toll on your mind and body, if you don't care for your physical well-being, it can make your mental health harder to support.

Along those same lines, incorporating gentle exercise into your routine can greatly benefit your overall well-being. Whether it's a short walk, yoga, or another form of physical activity, exercise can help release tension and improve your overall mood.

If your grief becomes overwhelming or if you're struggling to cope, consider seeking professional support. A therapist or counselor specializing in grief and pet loss can provide guidance and a safe space for you to explore your feelings.

When you're ready, find meaningful ways to honor and memorialize your pet. This could involve planting a tree, creating a memorial space, or making a donation to an animal charity in their name.

Remember that grieving is a unique and individual process, and there is no timeline for healing. It's okay to seek support and take the time you need to navigate this challenging period. By prioritizing self-care, you provide yourself with the compassion and strength necessary to move through grief and honor the memory of your beloved pet.

Following your beloved pet's departure, you will find yourself standing on the precipice of a moment forever etched in your heart—the moment of loss. The echoes of their presence linger in the spaces they once occupied, and the profound silence is a testament to the depth of our grief. In this delicate pause, we honor the journey we shared, acknowledging the beauty of the bond that transcended the boundaries of words and time.

As we turn the pages, the narrative unfolds into the next chapter, where the essence of mourning and memorializing takes center stage. In grief, we navigate the intricacies of emotions, finding solace in the memories that continue to paint our hearts with love. The journey through mourning is a sacred pilgrimage, a path where we pay homage to the cherished spirit that touched our lives in ways words cannot capture.

Let us move gently into this next chapter, where the canvas of remembrance awaits. In the midst of sorrow, we discover the transformative power of honoring and celebrating the legacy our pets leave behind. Together, we embark on a healing journey, embracing the tender moments of mourning and the timeless act of memorializing—a testament to the enduring love that forever binds us to our cherished companions.

CHAPTER SIX

Mourning and Memorializing

As we navigate the grief following the departure of our cherished pets, a chapter unfolds, one that invites us to traverse the delicate terrain of mourning and memorializing. In the aftermath of saying goodbye, we find ourselves standing on the threshold of remembrance—a space where the echoes of their presence linger, and the ache of loss meets the gentle balm of cherished memories.

This chapter is a contemplative journey through the emotional nuances of mourning and the transformative act of memorializing. Here, we embrace the ebb and flow of grief, recognizing it as a testament to the profound bond we shared with our four-legged companions. In the tender moments of mourning, we discover a sacred space where we honor our pets' irreplaceable role in our lives.

Join me as we explore the art of remembering, a tapestry woven with the threads of love, laughter, and the unique pawprints left on our hearts. Together, we navigate the healing path that mourning and memorializing unveil—a path that pays tribute to the enduring spirit of our beloved pets and celebrates the beauty they brought into our lives.

Honoring Your Pet's Memory

Honoring and memorializing a beloved pet is a deeply personal and meaningful process. It can give you a sense of purpose while feeling lost without your constant companion. Additionally, it can help you find closure and reach a state of acceptance. Here are various ways you can pay tribute to the enduring spirit of your furry friend:

- **Create a Memorial Space**: Designate a special area in your home or garden as a memorial space. Decorate it with a framed photo of your pet, their favorite toys, and perhaps a memorial plaque or stone.

- **Memorial Jewelry**: Consider getting a piece of memorial jewelry, such as a pendant or charm, that contains a small portion of your pet's ashes or fur. This wearable keepsake allows you to carry their memory with you.

- **Plant a Tree or Flowers**: Plant a tree, shrub, or flowers in memory of your pet. Watching new life grow in their honor can be a beautiful and symbolic way to celebrate their life.

- **Commemorative Artwork**: Commission or create artwork that captures the essence of your pet. This could be a painting, a sculpture, or even a custom piece of digital art that reflects their personality.

- **Create a Scrapbook**: Compile a scrapbook filled with photographs, anecdotes, and mementos that showcase the special moments you shared with your pet. This tangible keepsake can be a source of comfort and reflection.

- **Write a Letter**: Pen a heartfelt letter to your departed pet. Express your love, gratitude, and their impact on your life. Writing can be a therapeutic way to externalize your emotions.

- **Light a Memorial Candle**: Light a memorial candle on significant dates, such as their birthday or the anniversary of their passing. It becomes a symbolic gesture to honor their memory.

- **Hold a Memorial Service**: Organize a small memorial service with friends and family. Share stories and memories, and perhaps release biodegradable balloons or lanterns as a collective farewell gesture.

- **Donate in Their Name**: Donate to an animal charity, rescue organization, or veterinary clinic in your pet's name.

- **Create a Digital Tribute**: Craft a digital tribute in the form of a slideshow, video, or blog post that celebrates your pet's life. Share it with friends and family or within online pet communities.

- **Customized Headstone or Marker**: If your pet is buried, consider placing a customized headstone or marker at their resting place. Include their name, dates, and a special message that captures their essence.

- **Host a Celebration of Life**: Instead of focusing solely on the loss, consider hosting a celebration of your pet's life. Invite friends over for a gathering where you share happy memories, look through photos, and celebrate the joy your pet brought into your home.

- **Create a Pet Memorial Fund**: Establish a memorial fund in your pet's name. Contribute to it regularly, and use the fund to support pet-related causes or initiatives that align with your pet's passions.

Choose the methods that resonate most with you and align with your pet's personality. The goal is to create a lasting tribute that brings comfort, celebrates their life, and helps you navigate the journey of mourning in an authentic and healing way.

Moving Memorials

Many individuals and families have created moving memorials to pay tribute to their pets. These memorials offer solace and healing while bringing forth wonderful memories of their happiest times with their beloved fur babies.

The Memory Garden

After losing her faithful Labrador, Emma, Sarah created a memory garden in her backyard. She planted colorful flowers and placed a small bench beside a framed photo of Emma. It became a serene space where Sarah often sat, reflecting on their shared joyful moments.

The Paw Print Keepsake

Mark, a cat owner grieving the loss of his feline companion, Luna, decided to create a paw print keepsake. Using pet-safe ink, he carefully pressed Luna's paw onto a canvas. This tangible imprint now hangs in his home, serving as a cherished reminder of the gentle presence Luna brought into his life.

The Commemorative Artwork

When Rachel lost her adventurous parrot, Mango, she commissioned a local artist to create a vibrant painting capturing Mango's lively personality. The artwork now hangs prominently in her living room, as a colorful tribute to the feathery friend who filled her home with joy.

The Memorial Jewelry

After the passing of their beloved dog, Max, the Garcia family decided to turn a portion of his ashes into a memorial pendant. Each family member wears a piece of the pendant, creating a sense of connection and closeness even in Max's physical absence.

The Digital Memorial

Michael, a cat owner, created a digital memorial for his departed cat, Whiskers. He compiled photos and videos, sharing Whiskers' playful antics and endearing moments on a dedicated website. This digital tribute became a way to involve friends and family in celebrating Whiskers' life.

The Annual Candlelight Vigil

Emily, who shared her life with a loyal Golden Retriever named Buddy, organizes an annual candlelight vigil on the anniversary of Buddy's passing. Friends and neighbors gather, each holding a candle, to share stories and express their gratitude for the joy Buddy brought to their lives.

The Paw Print Walk

Mark and Lisa, mourning the loss of their cat, Muffin, organized a symbolic paw print walk in their neighborhood. Friends and family joined, creating colorful paw prints along the sidewalk in Muffin's memory. The event honored Muffin and raised funds for a local animal shelter.

The Communal Memorial Service

After the loss of their beloved rabbit, Thumper, the Thompson family held a communal memorial service in a nearby park. They invited other pet owners in the community to join, creating a space for shared grief and support. Each participant released a biodegradable balloon as a collective farewell gesture.

These stories illustrate the diverse and heartfelt ways people memorialize their pets. Through art, tangible keepsakes, digital tributes, or communal events, each method reflects the unique bond shared with a furry companion and the enduring desire to honor their memory.

Mourning Rituals and Traditions

Navigating the delicate journey of mourning a beloved pet is a process unique to each individual. The depth of the bond shared with our furry companions often prompts the creation of meaningful rituals and traditions to honor their memory. In the space of grief, consider these compassionate mourning rituals and traditions as gestures of love and remembrance.

Gather photographs, notes, and mementos in a dedicated scrapbook. Take the time to reminisce about the joyful moments shared with your pet. This tangible tribute becomes a visual narrative of their life, a cherished keepsake that can be revisited whenever you need to feel close to them.

You can also illuminate a special candle in honor of your pet. This simple yet poignant act can be performed on significant dates, during quiet moments of reflection, or as part of a memorial ceremony. The soft glow symbolizes the enduring light of their memory.

Cultivate a memorial garden with flowers, shrubs, or a tree to honor your pet. As you nurture these living symbols, you perpetuate the cycle of life and growth—a testament to your pet's enduring impact on your heart. The more time you spend in the garden, the closer you may feel to your beloved pet.

Consider wearing a piece of memorial jewelry that holds a small memento of your pet, such as fur or ashes. This wearable keepsake becomes a comforting and tangible connection, allowing you to carry a part of them with you.

Take intentional trips to places your pet loved. Whether it's a park, a beach, or a cozy corner of your home, spending time in these familiar spaces allows you to feel their presence and connect with the cherished memories you created together. While you're there, think back on all the fond memories you created together.

In the tender embrace of these mourning rituals and traditions, you are creating a sanctuary for your grief and paying homage to the enduring love you shared with your pet. Each gesture is a compassionate step forward on the path to healing, allowing the beauty of their memory to continue to enrich your life.

How to Create a Personalized Ritual

Creating a personalized ritual to honor the bond with your pet is a deeply meaningful and therapeutic process. This ritual serves as a unique expression of your love, allowing you to celebrate the memories, acknowledge the grief, and find solace in the enduring connection you shared.

When creating your ritual, consider the unique qualities and personality traits that defined your pet. Were they playful, gentle, adventurous, or loving? Reflecting on these characteristics will guide the elements you choose for your ritual.

Next, select a location that holds significance for you and your pet. It could be your home, a favorite park, a beach, or any place where you shared special moments. The familiarity of the setting enhances the ritual's emotional resonance.

You'll need to clarify the intention behind your ritual. Are you seeking closure, expressing gratitude, or simply celebrating the love you shared? Understanding the purpose will help shape the elements of the ritual.

Choose symbolic elements that represent your pet's life and the bond you shared. This could include candles, flowers, stones, or items that hold sentimental value. Each element should carry a meaning significant to your relationship.

As you develop a ceremony, ensure that it resonates with your emotions and memories. It can include moments of reflection, reading a heartfelt letter, playing your pet's favorite music, or reciting a poem. Tailor the ceremony to align with your pet's personality and the emotions you want to express.

If you feel comfortable, invite friends or family who shared a connection with your pet to participate in the ritual. Their presence can offer support and a shared acknowledgment of the love you all had for your furry companion. Do not feel obligated to involve anyone else, as this is a deeply personal experience for you.

Incorporate a segment where you and others, if included, present and share stories and memories about your pet. This sharing of anecdotes allows everyone to celebrate the joy your pet brought into their lives. Additionally, it can keep the event from turning too somber. While it is a ritual to remember a lost loved one, it doesn't need to be shrouded in sadness. After all, your pet brought you great joy during their life, so remembering them should, too.

Include a symbolic act that signifies the transition from grief to honoring your pet's memory. This could be lighting a candle, releasing balloons, planting a flower, or creating a piece of art. Choose an act that resonates with your emotions and intentions.

You can also document the ritual through photos, videos, or by creating a scrapbook. This serves as a lasting keepsake that can be revisited whenever you want to reconnect with the memories and emotions of the ritual.

Your personalized ritual is a deeply individual expression of grief and love. Allow yourself the freedom to adapt, modify, or improvise elements as needed. The goal is to create a meaningful experience that resonates with your heart.

Consider making your ritual an annual tradition to commemorate your pet's life. Each year, revisit the ceremony, allowing it to evolve and reflect the ongoing impact your pet has had on your life.

By crafting a personalized ritual, you are honoring your pet's memory and creating a space for healing and reflection. The authenticity of this ritual becomes a powerful tool for navigating grief and expressing the enduring love you hold for your furry friend.

In the echoes of our personalized rituals and tributes, we find solace in honoring and memorializing our beloved pets. Each candle lit, each flower planted, and every heartfelt word spoken becomes a testament to the enduring bond that transcends the boundaries of time and space. As we navigate this chapter dedicated to celebrating the lives of our cherished companions, we carry with us the warmth of shared memories and the gentle balm of love.

With the fragility of grief still lingering, we turn the page to the next chapter—a chapter that delves into the intricate landscape of coping with the profound loss of our furry confidants. Here, we explore the delicate nuances of grief, understanding how it ebbs and flows and uncovering the strategies that guide us through the healing journey. As we transition from memorializing to mourning, let us embrace the tenderness of our emotions, knowing that each tear shed is a testament to the profound love that forever binds us to our dear pets.

CHAPTER SEVEN

Coping With Grief

Following our beloved pet's departure, grief becomes a somewhat constant companion, and the landscape of our hearts is forever changed. This chapter is an exploration into the intricate terrain of coping with the profound loss of our furry companions. In the shadow of their absence, we navigate the nuanced emotions that grief unfurls, seeking solace and understanding amid heartache.

As we delve into the depths of sorrow, we embark on a journey of self-compassion, embracing the unique and often unpredictable waves of grief that wash over us. This chapter is a guide, a compassionate companion, offering insights into the intricate tapestry of emotions accompanying the loss of a pet. Together, we navigate the delicate balance of honoring our pain while cherishing the memories that continue to illuminate our hearts. Join me as we explore the transformative power of coping with grief, recognizing that healing patiently awaits within the tender threads of mourning.

Day-to-Day Coping Strategies

Navigating day-to-day activities while working through the grieving process of losing a pet can be a challenging but essential aspect of healing. As with any loss, you may struggle to do the things you used to do. Taking certain steps can help you cope and manage as you work your way through these challenges.

First, it's important to understand that grief is a unique and individual process. You must set realistic expectations for yourself and acknowledge that some days may be more difficult than others. Allow space for the ebb and flow of emotions without judgment.

Establishing a daily routine can provide a sense of structure and normalcy during a challenging time. Having a schedule helps create predictability, which can be comforting as you navigate through grief. If you know what you need to do next and when you need to do it, it can take pressure off your troubled mind.

While you're navigating grief, make self-care a priority. Attend to your physical and emotional well-being by getting enough sleep, eating nourishing meals, and engaging in activities that bring you comfort and joy.

Don't forget to reach out to friends, family, or support groups who understand the depth of your grief. Share your feelings, and don't hesitate to ask for support when needed. Connection can be a powerful source of comfort.

Don't erase all memories of your pet in an attempt to free yourself from the pain. Instead, integrate reminders of your pet in your living space. This could include placing a framed photo, keeping a favorite toy, or creating a small memorial area. Having these reminders can be both comforting and healing.

Always permit yourself to grieve throughout the day. Allow moments of sadness, and don't suppress your emotions. Grieving is a natural process, and acknowledging your feelings is an essential part of healing.

Recognize when you need to establish boundaries. If certain activities or conversations are too emotionally taxing, setting limits and communicating your needs to those around you is okay. Taking a break from social activities now and then may be exactly what you need to do to care for yourself.

While it's important to acknowledge your grief, engaging in activities that provide distraction can offer moments of relief. Whether it's reading, watching a movie, or pursuing a hobby, find healthy distractions that bring comfort.

Consider incorporating mindfulness techniques into your day. Take moments to breathe deeply, be present in the current moment, and cultivate a sense of gratitude for the time you shared with your pet. These practices will also keep you from getting locked into intense bouts of sadness. They will allow you to experience them and release them.

Take the time to establish new rituals that honor your pet's memory. This could include lighting a candle, saying a few words, or simply spending a few quiet moments in reflection each day. These rituals can be a soothing part of your routine.

If the grief ever becomes overwhelming, consider seeking the support of a therapist or counselor specializing in pet loss. Professional guidance can provide valuable tools for navigating the complexities of grief.

Take time each day to intentionally focus on positive memories of your pet. Celebrate the joy and companionship they brought into your life, allowing those memories to uplift and comfort you.

Remember, grief is a process that unfolds over time. Be patient and compassionate with yourself as you navigate day-to-day life. Each small step forward is a testament to your resilience and love for your beloved pet.

Handling Grief Triggers and Anniversaries

Handling grief triggers and significant events, such as anniversaries, requires a compassionate and proactive approach. Knowing what these triggers are and what types of events will cause a reaction is essential to prepare yourself for the situation. You can learn to guide yourself through the event with minimal upset or find ways to work around it.

When faced with grief triggers or anniversaries, acknowledge the emotions that arise. Accept that these feelings are a natural part of the grieving process. Give yourself permission to feel without judgment. As always, know that grief is nothing to be ashamed of. Even if you believe you are fully healed, a trigger can cause feelings to arise when you least expect it. Don't treat yourself harshly under these conditions, as it is a perfectly normal response.

A best practice is to anticipate upcoming triggers or anniversaries and plan how you want to approach them. Having a plan can help you feel more in control and prepared for the emotional impact of these events. Consider if you want to be alone or have support when the event occurs.

Consider establishing rituals or ceremonies that hold personal significance. This could include visiting your pet's resting place, lighting a candle, or engaging in activities that celebrate their life. Creating intentional rituals can bring a sense of purpose and connection that can help you ease past the pain caused by the trigger.

Don't hesitate to lean on your support network during challenging times. Share your feelings with friends, family, or a support group. Having someone to talk to can provide comfort and validation.

If certain traditions or activities trigger overwhelming emotions, consider modifying or adapting them. It's okay to create new rituals that better align with your current emotional needs. What you did yesterday with success doesn't have to be the same thing you do today. Our needs change as we grow and develop.

Writing down your thoughts and feelings in a journal can be a therapeutic way to process grief triggers. Expressing your emotions on paper provides a tangible outlet for your innermost thoughts. Your journal can be a private place to store these thoughts, or if you're comfortable, you can share it with those you love and trust.

During anniversaries or trigger events, give yourself the space to grieve. It's okay to take time off work, clear your schedule, or step away from commitments if needed. Prioritize your emotional well-being.

If the intensity of your emotions becomes overwhelming, consider seeking guidance from a grief counselor or therapist. Professional support can offer coping strategies tailored to your specific needs.

Surround yourself with a supportive environment. Be in spaces that bring you comfort and peace. Whether it's your home, a park, or a place connected to positive memories, choose environments that facilitate healing.

Use trigger events as an opportunity to focus on the positive aspects of your pet's life. Celebrate the joy they brought into your world and the love you shared. Redirecting your thoughts towards positive memories can be uplifting. Instead of dwelling solely on the loss, find ways to celebrate the positive milestones and memories you shared with your pet. Acknowledge the love and companionship that defined your relationship.

Above all, be gentle with yourself. Grieving is a process that unfolds over time, and healing takes patience. Allow yourself the grace to navigate these difficult moments without self-judgment.

Remember, everyone experiences grief differently, and there is no right or wrong way to navigate trigger events or anniversaries. By approaching these moments with self-compassion and utilizing supportive strategies, you can honor your pet's memory while gently moving through the waves of grief.

Finding Support

Finding support and community when managing pet loss is crucial for navigating the grieving process. Occasionally, family and friends may not be able to provide the support we need when recovering and healing from the loss of a pet. Many resources dedicated to pet loss grief exist, providing the needed support. You can choose the ideal solution based on your preferences.

- ASPCA Pet Loss Hotline: The ASPCA offers a Pet Loss Support Hotline at (877) GRIEF-10, providing free counseling and support for those grieving the loss of a pet.

- Online Support Groups:

  - Association for Pet Loss and Bereavement (APLB): APLB offers online support groups, forums, and resources for those coping with pet loss.

  - Pet Loss Grief Support Forum (Rainbows Bridge): Rainbows Bridge provides an online community where individuals can share their stories, offer support, and find comfort in a forum setting.

- Counseling Services

  - Pet Loss Counselors: Many therapists and grief counselors specialize in pet loss. Websites like Grief.com and Psychology Today allow you to search for counselors in your area who offer pet loss support.

  - University Veterinary Care Center (UVCC): UVCC provides a list of pet loss support resources, including counseling services.

- Local Veterinary Clinics: Your local veterinary clinic may have information on pet loss support groups or grief counseling services in your community. They can provide recommendations based on your location.

- Books on Pet Loss:

  - *The Loss of a Pet: A Guide to Coping with the Grieving Process When a Pet Dies* by Wallace Sife: This book offers guidance on coping with the loss of a pet and understanding the grieving process.

  - *Grieving the Death of a Pet* by Betty J. Carmack: Betty Carmack explores the emotional impact of losing a pet and provides practical strategies for healing.

- Pet Loss Websites and Resources:

  - Pet Loss Help: Pet Loss Help is a comprehensive website with articles, resources, and information on pet loss support groups.

  - Pet Loss Matters: This website offers articles, stories, and a directory of pet loss support services.

- Facebook Groups: Many pet loss support groups exist on Facebook. Search for groups like "Pet Loss Support" or "Grieving the Loss of a Pet" to connect with others who are experiencing similar emotions.

- Local Animal Shelters and Rescues: Local animal shelters and rescue organizations may have information on grief support services or events in your community.

Remember, seeking support is a sign of strength, and connecting with others who understand the unique bond between humans and pets can be profoundly healing. Reach out to these resources to find the support you need during this challenging time.

Stories of Finding Support

Many individuals have reached out to their community for support following the loss of a pet. The various resources available have proven to be highly effective and beneficial.

Online Support Group Comforts Carla

Carla, devastated by the sudden loss of her cat, found solace in an online pet loss support group. Carla felt a sense of understanding and connection through sharing her grief and reading the stories of others who had experienced similar pain. The support group became a virtual sanctuary where members offered compassion, empathy, and practical advice on navigating the grieving process.

Local Pet Loss Counseling Offers Guidance to Mark

Mark sought the guidance of a local pet loss counselor after losing his faithful dog. The counselor provided a safe space for Mark to express his emotions and navigate the complexities of grief. Through one-on-one sessions, Mark learned coping strategies, found validation for his feelings, and gradually discovered a path toward healing.

Community Pet Memorial Event Brings Together Maria and Jake

Marking the loss of her parrot, Maria attended a community pet memorial event organized by a local animal shelter. There, she met Jake, who had recently lost his dog. The event facilitated an environment where pet owners shared stories, created art in memory of their pets, and found a sense of community. Maria and Jake formed a lasting connection, offering each other understanding and support.

Facebook Group Provides Comfort to Sarah

Sarah, grieving the loss of her cat, joined a Facebook group dedicated to pet loss support. Members shared coping strategies, uplifting stories, and words of encouragement. The group became a virtual haven where Sarah felt understood and less alone in her journey through grief. The ongoing support and sense of community helped her navigate the challenging emotional landscape.

Local Veterinarian Clinic Organizes Grief Support Sessions for Tom

Tom, struggling with the loss of his dog, discovered that his local veterinarian clinic offered grief support sessions. Attending these sessions allowed him to connect with others facing similar struggles. The veterinary team provided medical and emotional support, offering resources and guidance to help Tom navigate the grieving process.

These stories underscore the profound impact that support networks can have on pet owners coping with the loss of their furry friends.

Whether through online communities, local counseling services, or community events, the shared understanding and empathy within these networks create a space where grief can be expressed, validated, and gradually transformed into a journey of healing.

As we gently conclude this chapter on coping with grief over the loss of a cherished pet, we recognize the unique and tender journey each individual undertakes. The path of grief is not linear; it meanders through moments of pain, reflection, and eventual healing. Through shared stories, strategies, and the embrace of support networks, we have explored the multifaceted nature of mourning our beloved companions.

As we turn the page, we delve into a new chapter—one that delicately addresses the intricacies of talking to children about pet loss, providing solace to other pets who share our homes, and navigating the delicate task of conveying our feelings to family and friends. This chapter acknowledges the ripple effects of pet loss within our households and communities, offering insights and guidance on navigating these interconnected aspects of the grieving process. Together, let us embark on this empathetic exploration, recognizing that the threads of love and understanding weave seamlessly through the fabric of our shared experiences.

CHAPTER EIGHT

Family, Friends, and Other Pets

The chapter we explore now is one that delicately weaves through the shared spaces of both children and our faithful animal companions. Loss touches each member of our households uniquely, and in this chapter, we will embark on a journey, offering solace to the tender hearts of our children and the loyal paws of our other pets.

Children, with their innocent eyes and open hearts, often grapple with the complexities of grief in a way that's both profound and delicate. Likewise, our four-legged friends, who have shared in the joys and companionship of their departed sibling, need a guiding hand through the labyrinth of emotions that follows the loss.

We'll explore strategies and insights to help children understand and process grief, offering them a safe space for expression and healing. Simultaneously, we'll delve into the world of our other pets, providing guidance on fostering a supportive environment where they can adapt to the changes in their furry family.

Expressing our grief to friends and family is another aspect we'll explore in this chapter. In times of sorrow, communication becomes a bridge that connects hearts, allowing for mutual understanding and support. We'll discuss effective ways to convey our feelings, helping our loved ones comprehend the depth of our grief and providing a foundation for empathy.

Together, let us embark on this journey of nurturing hearts and guiding paws, recognizing that through shared compassion, we can illuminate the path toward healing for both our human and animal companions.

Talking to Children About Pet Loss

Explaining pet loss to children at different developmental stages requires thoughtful communication and sensitivity. Depending on their age, you'll need to use specific tactics when addressing children. Comprehension comes at much different levels. However, one thing is the same, no matter the age, always be direct and don't use terms that can be confusing.

Addressing

Preschoolers (Ages 2-5)

Keep things simple by using simple and concrete language to explain that the pet has passed away. Avoid using confusing or abstract terms.

For example, instead of saying the pet is "sleeping," use language like "the pet's body stopped working."

Focus on using soft and gentle imagery to describe the situation, such as the pet going to a special place or becoming a star in the sky. Reassure them that the pet is not in pain and that their love for the pet remains.

You should encourage them to express their feelings. Acknowledge their sadness and let them know it's okay to cry. Share your own emotions to show that grieving is a natural part of the process.

Addressing

School-Age Children (Ages 6-12)

Provide straightforward information about death. Use age-appropriate terms and avoid euphemisms. Explain that death is a natural part of life and that the pet won't be coming back.

Encourage them to express their emotions through talking, drawing, or writing. Offer a safe space for them to share memories. Validate their grief and let them know that everyone mourns in their own way.

Be prepared for questions about the afterlife, and answer honestly based on your family's beliefs. Use language that aligns with your values.

Addressing

Teenagers (Ages 13-18)

Respect their need for space. Teenagers may process grief more independently, but let them know you're available if they want to talk. Share your own feelings and experiences, fostering a sense of connection.

If applicable, involve them in decisions about memorializing the pet or handling the remains. This can provide a sense of control during a challenging time. Offer options for creating a memorial or participating in a ceremony if they are interested.

Discuss healthy coping strategies, such as journaling, art, or engaging in activities they enjoy. Encourage them to seek support from friends, family, or counseling if needed.

General Tips for All Ages

Some things will be the same regardless of the age of the child. You can use these general tips:

- Utilize books, videos, or online resources designed for their age group to help explain the concept of death and grief.

- Stick to regular routines as much as possible. Predictability can provide comfort during times of upheaval.

- Consider creating a memorial or ritual to honor the pet's memory. This can be especially helpful for children who benefit from tangible ways to express their feelings.

- Reassure children that the love for the pet will always remain.

- Emphasize that memories of the pet will live on in their hearts.

- Grieving is a process that takes time. Be patient and provide ongoing support as children navigate their feelings.

Remember that every child is unique, and these suggestions are general guidelines. Tailor your approach based on your child's personality, preferences, and individual needs.

Strategies to Support Children Through Their Grief

Supporting children through grief involves providing comfort, understanding, and a safe space for them to express their emotions. Here are strategies to help guide children through the grieving process:

- **Encourage Expression**: Create an open environment where children feel comfortable expressing their feelings. Encourage them to talk, draw, write, or engage in activities that allow them to express their grief.

- **Validate Their Emotions**: Acknowledge and validate their emotions. Let them know it's normal to feel a range of emotions, including sadness, anger, confusion, or even relief.

- **Answer Questions Honestly**: Be honest and age-appropriate when answering their questions about death. Use simple language and provide information based on their developmental level.

- **Share Your Own Feelings**: Share your own emotions and

experiences with grief. Modeling healthy expressions of feelings helps normalize the grieving process.

- **Maintain Routine**: Keep regular routines as much as possible. Consistency provides a sense of stability during a time of emotional upheaval.

- **Create a Memorial**: Involve children in creating a memorial for the pet. This could include making a scrapbook, planting a tree, or drawing. Having a tangible way to remember the pet can be comforting.

- **Read Books on Grief**: Choose age-appropriate books that discuss pet loss and grief. Reading together can provide a platform for discussing emotions and normalizing the grieving process.

- **Involve Them in Rituals**: If your family has specific rituals or ceremonies to honor the pet, involve the children. This can include a small ceremony, lighting a candle, or creating a memorial space in the home.

- **Seek Professional Support**: If you notice prolonged or intense grief reactions, consider seeking the support of a grief counselor or therapist experienced in working with children. Professional guidance can offer coping strategies and a safe space for them to process their emotions.

- **Encourage Positive Memories**: Reminisce about positive memories with the pet. Encourage children to share their favorite moments, creating a positive narrative around the pet's life.

- **Use Art and Play Therapy**: For younger children, art and play therapy can help them effectively process grief. Provide art supplies or toys that allow them to express themselves nonverbally.

- **Monitor Changes in Behavior**: Be attentive to changes in behavior, sleep patterns, or academic performance. Significant changes may indicate a need for additional support or professional intervention.

- **Involve Them in Decision-Making**: If applicable, involve children in decisions related to the pet's passing, such as choosing a burial option or deciding on a memorial. This involvement can provide a sense of control.

- **Connect with Support Groups**: If available, consider joining a pet loss support group specifically designed for children. Connecting with peers who share similar experiences can be comforting.

Remember that grief is a unique process for each child, and they may respond differently based on their age, personality, and previous experiences with loss. Providing ongoing support, patience, and understanding is key to helping children navigate their grief in a healthy way.

The Impact on Other Pets

Pet loss can significantly impact surviving pets, as they often form deep bonds with their animal companions. Understanding and addressing the effects of pet loss on these animals is crucial for their well-being.

Like humans, animals experience grief and mourning. Surviving pets may exhibit signs of sadness, anxiety, or confusion after the loss of a companion. They may search for the missing pet, vocalize more, or become less active.

Behavioral changes are common in surviving pets. They may become withdrawn, exhibit changes in eating habits, or demonstrate a lack of interest in activities they once enjoyed. Some pets may become more clingy or show signs of restlessness.

The presence of a companion animal provides a sense of routine and stability for pets. The loss disrupts this routine, and surviving pets may experience stress or uncertainty as they adapt to the changes in their environment.

The stress of losing a companion can impact the physical health of surviving pets. Some may experience a decline in overall health, changes in appetite, or susceptibility to illnesses due to a weakened immune system.

Pets that were closely bonded may suffer from separation anxiety after the loss of their companion. They may exhibit distress when left alone, leading to destructive behaviors or excessive vocalization.

In households with multiple pets, the loss of one can alter the social dynamics among the surviving animals. Establishing new hierarchies or adapting to the absence of a specific playmate may take time.

Pets can experience depression in response to the loss of a companion. Signs may include lethargy, a lack of interest in surroundings, and decreased overall activity. Some surviving pets may seek increased attention from their human caregivers to compensate for the loss of companionship from their furry friend. They may become more attached and demand more interaction.

Changes in vocalization patterns, including increased meowing or barking, can be a sign of distress in surviving pets. They may be expressing a need for comfort or companionship.

The stress of losing a companion can have a lasting impact on surviving pets. It's essential to monitor their well-being and provide additional support as needed to help them adjust.

To support surviving pets through the grieving process:

- **Maintain Routine**: Stick to a consistent routine to provide a sense of stability.

- **Offer Comfort**: Provide extra attention, affection, and comfort to reassure them.

- **Provide Distractions**: Engage them in activities and play to distract them from grief.

- **Introduce New Companionship Gradually**: If considering a new pet, introduce them gradually to avoid overwhelming the surviving pet.

If behavioral changes persist or worsen, seeking guidance from a veterinarian or animal behaviorist may be beneficial to ensure the well-being of the surviving pet.

Guiding Your Surviving Pets Through Grief

Helping other pets through the transition after losing a companion involves understanding their unique needs and providing support as they navigate the changes in their environment and social dynamics. Pay close attention to the behavior of the surviving pets. Each pet may react differently to the loss, and understanding their individual responses is the first step in providing appropriate support.

Stick to a consistent routine to provide a sense of stability for the surviving pets. Regular feeding times, walks, and play sessions can help create predictability in their daily lives. Altering their routines could introduce too much change at one time.

Offer additional attention and affection to the surviving pets. Spend quality time with them, engage in interactive play, and provide comfort through gentle touch.

Introduce items with the scent of the departed pet to help surviving pets recognize and adjust to the absence. This can be a blanket or a toy that belonged to the lost companion. Designate safe and comfortable spaces for the surviving pets. Having a cozy retreat where they can relax and feel secure can be especially important during times of adjustment.

If the surviving pets were part of a multi-pet household, encourage positive social interactions. Engage them in joint activities and monitor their interactions to ensure a healthy social dynamic. Offer toys, puzzles, or activities that can serve as distractions for the surviving pets. Engaging them in play can help redirect their focus and alleviate stress.

Keep an eye on their eating habits. Grief can sometimes affect appetite, and changes in eating patterns may indicate emotional distress. If necessary, consult with a veterinarian for guidance. Be on the lookout for signs of weight loss and excessive sleeping, as these could be signs of health complications from the grieving process.

If contemplating bringing a new pet into the household, introduce the new companion gradually and cautiously. Allow the surviving pets time to adjust to the new addition at their own pace. Of course, this slow transition is true anytime you introduce a new pet. However, following the loss of a beloved companion, the adjustment could take significantly longer.

Consult with a veterinarian if you notice persistent changes in behavior, appetite, or overall well-being. They can provide guidance on managing stress and ensuring the health of your surviving pets.

Offer comfort items, such as a cozy bed, favorite toys, or blankets, to create a familiar and reassuring environment for the surviving pets. Reassure the surviving pets through soothing words and gentle actions. Your presence and comfort can go a long way in helping them feel secure during the transition.

Remember, the grieving process extends to pets, and they may need time to adjust to the changes in their social structure. Providing love, attention, and understanding will aid them in navigating the transition and finding comfort in the midst of loss.

Responding to Family and Friends

Communicating your grief needs to family and friends is a crucial aspect of receiving the support and understanding you require during a challenging time. Not everyone will fully understand how you feel or the bond you had with your pet. Being able to effectively communicate your feelings is essential to conveying your needs.

Before communicating with others, take some time to reflect on your own needs. Consider the kind of support you find most helpful, whether it's someone to talk to, practical assistance, or simply companionship.

Find an appropriate time and setting to discuss your grief needs. Choose a calm and private space where you can have an open and honest conversation without distractions.

Express your feelings openly and honestly. Be direct about your needs and let your loved ones know how they can best support you. Honest communication sets the foundation for understanding.

Provide specific examples of how others can support you. Clear requests can guide their actions, whether it's someone to listen to you without judgment, help with daily tasks, or accompany you during difficult moments.

Some people may not fully understand the depth of grief and the support needed. Share resources or information about grief to help them comprehend the emotional and physical toll it can take.

Let your family and friends know if you're experiencing changes in your behavior or if certain situations are particularly challenging for you. This insight helps them understand your needs better.

Frame your needs using "I" statements to avoid sounding accusatory. For example, say, "I would appreciate it if you could check in on me regularly" instead of "You never check in on me." Recognize that people have different ways of grieving, and their expressions of support may vary. Acknowledge these differences while conveying your specific needs. Clearly communicate any boundaries you may need during this time. Establishing boundaries is essential, whether it's alone time, specific topics to avoid, or the need for occasional company.

Understand that others may not fully grasp your needs immediately. Be patient and open to reiterating your requests as necessary. Grief is an evolving process, and your needs may change over time.

Encourage your loved ones to express their concerns or questions. Open communication fosters understanding and allows for a supportive dialogue.

If communication becomes challenging, consider seeking the assistance of a grief counselor or therapist together. Professional guidance can help facilitate a constructive conversation about your needs.

Remember that your family and friends may genuinely want to support you but might not know how best to do so. By expressing your grief needs with clarity, empathy, and patience, you create a foundation for a supportive network that can help you navigate the complexities of grief.

How to Handle Insensitive Remarks or Misunderstandings About Pet Grief

Dealing with insensitive remarks or misunderstandings about pet loss grief can be challenging, but there are ways to navigate these situations with grace and assertiveness. While they may hurt in the heat of the moment, when you reflect back on them, you'll likely find that the person issuing the remark genuinely meant no harm. Pet grief is not always well-understood by others, leaving room for significant misunderstandings.

Allow yourself to feel the emotions that arise when faced with insensitive remarks. It's okay to feel hurt, angry, or frustrated. Acknowledging your emotions is the first step in processing them.

Some people may not fully understand the depth of the bond between humans and their pets. If you feel comfortable, take the opportunity to educate them about the significance of pet relationships and the grief that follows their loss.

Establish clear boundaries regarding what comments or questions are acceptable. If someone crosses these boundaries, calmly but assertively communicate that you'd prefer not to discuss certain aspects of your grief.

If someone unknowingly says something hurtful, express your feelings and let them know how their words impacted you. Use "I" statements to avoid sounding accusatory and focus on your emotions.

Seek the company of friends, family, or support groups who understand and empathize with your grief. Being around those who offer comfort and validation can help counteract insensitive remarks. Surround yourself with individuals who respect and honor your feelings. Share your experiences with those who genuinely understand the depth of your grief.

In some cases, injecting humor can be a coping mechanism. If the comment is unintentionally insensitive, gently redirect the conversation with humor if it feels appropriate to do so. If someone brings up a topic that you find uncomfortable, gently redirect the conversation to a more neutral or positive subject. This helps shift the focus away from potentially hurtful remarks.

Engage in self-care activities that bring comfort and solace. Whether it's spending time with supportive friends, practicing mindfulness, or enjoying a hobby, prioritize activities that contribute to your well-being.

Join online pet loss support groups where you can connect with individuals who share similar experiences. These communities provide a space to express your feelings without fear of judgment.

Understand that people may not always grasp the depth of your grief, and their comments may stem from a lack of understanding rather than malice. Recognize that your grief is a personal and valid experience.

If insensitive remarks significantly impact your well-being, consider seeking the support of a grief counselor or therapist. Professional guidance can provide coping strategies and a safe space to process your emotions.

Remember, it's okay to advocate for yourself and set boundaries when it comes to discussing your grief. Surrounding yourself with understanding and compassionate individuals can make a significant difference in navigating the complexities of pet loss grief.

We've explored the delicate journey of helping children and other pets navigate the profound loss of a beloved companion. Understanding the unique needs of each member of your household during this time is an essential step toward healing.

The bond between humans, pets, and their furry companions is a beautiful blend of shared moments, love, and irreplaceable memories. As we turn the page, let us embark on a new chapter that gently guides us on moving forward after the loss. Through insights, coping strategies, and the resilience that emerges from shared grief, we'll explore the path toward finding meaning, honoring memories, and embracing the healing that comes with time.

In the face of loss, there is an opportunity for growth, and in the chapters that follow, we'll navigate this transformative journey together, acknowledging the pain of goodbyes while embracing the promise of new beginnings.

Chapter Nine

Moving Forward

As we turn the pages of our journey through pet loss, we turn our focus toward the delicate art of moving forward after saying our tearful goodbyes. In the echoes of loss, we discover the strength to embrace new beginnings, acknowledging that the love we shared with our departed companions transcends the boundaries of time.

This chapter is a guide through the landscape of adjustment, where we learn to navigate the rhythm of life without the familiar presence of our cherished pets. It's a journey that encourages us to find resilience amid the void, acknowledging that healing is gradual.

We will explore the consideration of welcoming a new pet into our lives—a decision intertwined with hope and the prospect of creating fresh bonds. Once stretched by love, the heart has the capacity to expand and welcome new companions, each with their unique charm and spirit.

Maintaining the bond with the departed holds a sacred place in this chapter. We'll delve into ways to honor the memories, celebrate the shared moments, and keep the flame of love alive. For even in their absence, our pets continue to shape our lives, leaving pawprints on our hearts.

As we traverse the terrain of moving forward, let us open our hearts to the possibilities that await—a tapestry of resilience, remembrance, and the enduring love that transcends the boundaries between this world and the next.

Adjusting to Life Without Your Pet

Adjusting to a new normal without your cherished pet by your side is an emotional journey that requires patience, self-compassion, and an acknowledgment of the unique bond you shared. While you are constantly moving forward, you will still be in a place of healing. It is a continual progression and should not be rushed.

Grieving is a natural and essential part of adjusting to life without your pet. Allow yourself the time and space to feel the depth of your emotions. It's okay to mourn and reflect on the beautiful moments you shared.

Continue the rituals and routines you shared with your pet, even in their absence. Whether it's a daily walk, a specific feeding time, or a bedtime routine, maintaining these rituals can help maintain a sense of connection. Establishing a routine can provide a sense of normalcy. Plan your day with activities that bring you comfort and joy. The structure can be grounding during times of change.

Talk about your pet with friends, family, or a support group. Expressing your emotions and sharing memories can be therapeutic. Don't shy away from celebrating the joy they brought into your life. If the grief feels overwhelming, consider seeking the support of a grief counselor. Professional guidance can offer coping strategies and provide a safe space to navigate complex emotions.

Engage in a memorial project as a tribute to your pet. This could be creating a scrapbook, writing a letter, or even planting a tree in their honor. It's a beautiful way to channel your emotions into a tangible expression of love.

Prioritize self-care as you navigate this new normal. Take time for activities that bring you joy, whether reading, spending time in nature, or engaging in creative pursuits.

While the pain of loss is profound, consider opening your heart to new connections, whether furry or human. Adopting a new pet or volunteering at an animal shelter can be a way to honor your pet's legacy while embracing the possibility of new bonds.

Adjusting to life without your pet is a personal and evolving process. Be patient with yourself, cherish the memories, and allow the love you shared to guide you forward on this healing journey.

How to Incorporate Your Pet's Memory Into Your Daily Life

Incorporating the memory of a beloved pet into daily life is a beautiful way to honor their legacy and keep their spirit alive. Additionally, these memories can help fill the void left by losing your pet. Adding happy memories to your surroundings can help keep your experience moving toward a positive, healing light.

Start by integrating your pet's belongings into your daily surroundings. Keep their collar, a favorite blanket, or a special toy in a visible place. Touching these items can evoke comforting memories and a sense of connection. If you work in an office setting, you can even bring something small and place it on your desk to have a constant reminder of all the good times.

If your pet had a specific routine, continue aspects of it as a tribute. Whether it's their feeding schedule, a daily walk, or playtime, maintaining these rituals can provide a sense of continuity and closeness.

Craft or commission art that celebrates your pet's memory. This could be a custom portrait, a paw print keepsake, or even a piece of jewelry containing a small memento. These tangible reminders can be cherished and worn daily.

Express your feelings through writing. Consider writing letters to your pet or journaling about the moments you shared. This reflective practice lets you keep your pet's memory alive and process your emotions.

Continue to speak about your pet and incorporate their name into daily conversations. Share anecdotes, funny stories, or fond memories with friends and family, keeping their spirit alive through storytelling.

Acknowledge and celebrate special dates like their birthday, adoption day, or the anniversary of their passing. Light a candle, donate to an animal charity in their name, or perform a ritual that holds personal meaning.

Compile a digital photo album with pictures and videos of your pet. Browse through it regularly, sharing memories with loved ones and relishing in the visual representation of your time together.

Start a memory jar where you jot down special moments and memories. Whenever you miss your pet, revisit these notes. Over time, the jar becomes a collection of the joy they brought into your life.

Incorporating the memory of your beloved pet into your daily life is a deeply personal and healing process. These small yet meaningful gestures allow you to keep their spirit alive, finding solace in the enduring love and connection you shared.

Considering Another Pet

As we move through the rocky terrain of pet loss, there inevitably comes a moment when the heart begins to ponder the idea of welcoming a new furry friend into our lives. The emotional considerations of this decision are profound, requiring a delicate balance between honoring the past and embracing the potential for new connections.

In the wake of loss, the prospect of a new pet can serve as a beacon of hope—a living testament to the resilience of the heart. However, the decision to open our homes to a new companion is a deeply personal one, entwined with complex emotions.

Understanding the Emotional Landscape

Many pet owners grapple with feelings of guilt, questioning whether bringing a new pet into their lives is a betrayal of the memory of their departed friend. It's crucial to recognize that love is expansive; it can embrace both the past and the future.

A common concern is the fear of comparing a new pet to the one we lost. Each animal is unique, and acknowledging this individuality is essential for fostering a genuine connection. It's important to remember that no pet will ever truly replace the one that has been lost. However, that doesn't mean new bonds cannot be formed.

Knowing when the time is right is a nuanced consideration. Rushing into the decision may hinder the healing process while waiting too long might delay the potential joy and companionship a new pet can bring.

Recognizing the Signs: When It's Time for a New Beginning

When the intensity of grief begins to subside and the pain transforms into cherished memories, it may signal that your heart is opening up to the possibility of a new connection. If you're still deep in the waves of grief, it's likely not the ideal time to select a new friend and companion. You may not have the emotional capacity to provide them the love and care they need.

Assess your emotional readiness. If the idea of bringing a new pet into your life brings a sense of joy rather than guilt, it might indicate that you're emotionally prepared for this next chapter. However, no matter how far you've progressed through the grieving process, there may always be some level of guilt experienced when contemplating bringing home a new pet.

The decision to bring a new pet home requires time, commitment, and energy. It could be the right time if you find yourself willing and able to invest in building a new relationship.

Reflect on your departed pet's legacy. If the memories bring more smiles than tears, and you can envision incorporating those memories into a new bond, it may be a sign of readiness.

Approach the idea with an open heart. Understand that the new pet will bring its own personality, quirks, and charm. Embrace the prospect of a unique connection, one that complements but does not replace.

In the void between grief and renewal, the decision to bring a new pet into our lives is a continuation of a journey that encapsulates the profound love we hold for our departed companions. As we embark on this journey, may our hearts remain open, weaving a tapestry that honors the past while embracing the boundless capacity for love that the future holds.

Continuing Bonds

The love we share with our pets transcends the physical realm. As we navigate the intricate landscapes of grief and healing, the concept of maintaining a psychological bond with a deceased pet emerges as a source of solace and continuity. We will delve into the profound nature of this connection and how it continues to shape our lives.

The Intangible Thread of Connection

Memories serve as anchors that tether us to the essence of our departed companions. They are the threads that weave a tapestry of shared experiences, laughter, and unconditional love.

The psychological bond often manifests in continuing conversations with our pets. Whether in moments of solitude or during daily routines, speaking to them becomes a means of preserving the connection and seeking comfort.

Symbolic representations, such as keeping a photo or a paw print, act as tangible reminders of the psychological bond. Touching these objects can evoke a sense of closeness and provide a visual anchor to cherished memories.

Some individuals report experiencing dreams where their deceased pets visit them. These dream encounters can bring a sense of reassurance and a feeling of continued connection.

Navigating the Emotional Landscape

Maintaining a psychological bond with a deceased pet is a nuanced relationship between grief and healing. It's an acknowledgment that the emotional connection endures while the physical presence is no longer.

Honoring the legacy of our pets involves integrating their presence into our daily lives. Whether through rituals, keeping their belongings, or engaging in activities they enjoyed, these actions pay homage to their lasting impact.

Freely talking about our deceased pets keeps their memory alive. Sharing stories, anecdotes, and the love we still feel for them with friends and family ensures that their presence remains an integral part of our narrative.

Some find solace in seeking signs or signals that their pets are still with them in spirit. These moments can reinforce the psychological bond, whether it's a subtle presence, a familiar scent, or an unexplained occurrence.

Coping with Challenges

The journey of maintaining a psychological bond includes navigating the waves of grief that may resurface. Understanding that grief is dynamic and allowing oneself to experience these waves is a crucial aspect of the process.

Striking a balance between maintaining the psychological bond and allowing space for new connections is a delicate task. It involves honoring the past while embracing the potential for growth and new relationships.

The psychological bond with a deceased pet attests to the enduring nature of love. As we continue to cherish, remember, and engage with the essence of our departed companions, their impact remains etched in the very fabric of our being. In this enduring connection, we find a source of strength, solace, and a timeless reminder that love knows no boundaries—even those of life and death.

Narratives of Enduring Love

In the mosaic of grief and healing, the tales of those who have navigated the delicate balance of maintaining a psychological bond with their departed pets provide both inspiration and solace. As we weave through these narratives, we witness the evolution of love beyond the confines of time and space.

Echoes in the Garden

Sarah, an avid gardener, lost her beloved cat, Peanut. She dedicated a corner of her garden to keep the memory alive to him. She felt his presence as she tended to the plants, a whispered reminder of the joy he found in chasing butterflies. The evolving bond with Peanut became intertwined with the flourishing blossoms and the soft rustle of leaves—a testament to the enduring connection between a soul and the earth it once roamed.

The Art of Remembrance

John, an artist, found solace in creating portraits of his departed dog, Max. Each brush stroke seemed to capture Max's spirit, and the painting became a meditative ritual. As the portraits adorned the walls, they became more than depictions; they became portals through which John continued to engage with Max's energy, keeping their bond alive in the vibrant strokes of color.

Dream Journeys

Kelly experienced vivid dreams of her departed parrot, Sebastian. In these dreams, Sebastian would perch on her shoulder, preening her hair, and chirp familiar tunes. The dreams became a source of comfort, a nightly reunion transcending the boundaries of the waking world.

Through these dream journeys, Kelly felt Sebastian's continued presence, an ethereal dance that mirrored their shared days' rhythm.

Conversations Across Time

Kevin, after losing his Labrador, Buddy, found solace in talking to an empty chair where Buddy used to sit. The one-sided conversations became a therapeutic practice, a space where Mark could share his thoughts, joys, and sorrows. In this dialogue across time, he felt Buddy's invisible but palpable presence, offering a sense of companionship that transcended the physical realm.

Symbolic Tokens

For Ida, keeping a symbolic token—a paw print encased in a glass pendant—became a cherished ritual. Wearing it daily, she felt a subtle weight against her heart, a comforting reminder of the bond she shared with her departed rabbit, Teddy. The pendant became a tangible symbol of their enduring connection, a touchstone that grounded her in moments of solitude.

The Legacy of Laughter

After the loss of his mischievous cat, Fox, Cory discovered that humor was the bridge between grief and fond remembrance. He compiled a "Book of Fox," chronicling the cat's playful antics and hilarious escapades. As Cory revisited the pages, laughter became a vessel for the continued connection, a joyful echo of the irrepressible spirit that once filled his home.

These deeply illustrate the human-pet relationships, demonstrating that the bond with our departed companions is not confined to the past. Instead, it evolves, transforms, and manifests in myriad ways, offering a timeless connection that transcends the physical boundaries of life and death. As we continue to navigate the chapters of our lives, these narratives serve as beacons, guiding us towards the enduring power of love—the kind that echoes in gardens, dances in dreams, and finds expression in the art of remembrance.

This chapter has unraveled the threads of moving forward after the profound loss of a cherished pet. As we conclude, let us reflect on the essence of this journey—a journey marked by resilience, remembrance, and the unwavering love that persists even in the face of goodbyes.

In the ebb and flow of emotions, we've explored the intricacies of adjusting to a new normal, considering the prospect of a new pet, and maintaining the bond with the departed. Each revelation, each shared experience, is a stitch in the tapestry of resilience—a testament to the human spirit's capacity to heal, evolve, and find joy once more.

As we navigate the path of moving forward, we recognize that love is a continuum—a force that extends beyond the temporal boundaries of life. The decision to welcome a new companion is not a farewell to the love we held for our departed friend; instead, it's an acknowledgment that our hearts have the capacity to expand, embrace, and weave new connections while cherishing the imprints of the past.

Moving forward is not about leaving the memories behind but about carrying them forward as cherished legacies. Whether through memorial gardens, symbolic tokens, or continuing rituals, we honor the legacy of our pets, ensuring that their impact remains an integral part of our journey.

In the embrace of new beginnings, we find a chapter unfolding—an unwritten narrative filled with possibilities, growth, and the promise of fresh companionship. The stories shared by others who have traversed this path illuminate the way, showing that love persists, evolves, and finds expression in the laughter, dreams, and creative endeavors that shape our lives.

As we conclude this chapter, let us carry forward the lessons of resilience, the echoes of shared narratives, and the understanding that moving forward is not a linear journey but a nuanced exploration of love's enduring nature. May we find solace in the continuity of connection, celebrate the joy that new companions bring, and hold dear the memories that shape our hearts.

Moving forward after pet loss is a transition—an acknowledgment that life, with its twists and turns, continues. It is not a goodbye to the love we once knew but an invitation to embrace the unfolding chapters with open hearts. In the chapters that follow, we will explore the nuances of mourning, memorializing, and coping with grief, recognizing that each step is a part of the profound and transformative journey of healing.

CHAPTER TEN

Conclusion

Throughout the pages of this book, we've covered several important ways to understand and cope with pet loss and grief. While grief is challenging and a profoundly moving experience, having knowledge of its effects and how you can navigate the loss of a pet will help you move through the process. Keep these key takeaways in mind:

- The connection between humans and their pets is profound, characterized by unconditional love, companionship, and shared moments that create lasting bonds.

- Pet loss grief is a unique and complex experience, often underestimated by those who haven't experienced a deep connection with a furry companion.

- Pets play multifaceted roles in our lives, serving as companions, confidants, sources of joy, and therapeutic allies.

- The loss of a pet profoundly impacts emotional and physical well-being, influencing daily routines, relationships, and overall life satisfaction.

- The psychological connection with pets is significant, involving emotional attachment, companionship, and a sense of purpose and responsibility.

- Pet loss grief can manifest in various ways, including sadness, guilt, anger, and even physical symptoms. Acknowledging these manifestations is essential for effective coping.

- The stages of grief—denial, anger, bargaining, depression, and acceptance—apply to pet loss, but the process is unique and may not follow a linear trajectory.

- Pet owners may experience grief uniquely, influenced by the deep emotional connection, the absence of societal rituals, and the sometimes-unrecognized intensity of their loss.

- It's crucial to affirm that pet grief is normal, valid, and deserving of empathy and understanding from both oneself and others.

- Real-life stories illustrate the depth of human-pet relationships, demonstrating the significant impact of pet loss on individuals' lives.

- Complicated grief may arise, characterized by persistent, intense symptoms hindering daily functioning. Identifying signs and seeking professional help is crucial in such cases.

- Coping with pet loss involves acknowledging the pain, expressing emotions, creating memorials, seeking support, and considering rituals or activities that honor the pet's memory.

- Deciding to welcome a new pet involves emotional readiness, easing of grief intensity, willingness to invest time and energy, and open-heartedness to a unique connection.

- The psychological bond with a deceased pet can be sustained through memories, continuing conversations, symbolic representations, dream visits, and honoring their legacy.

- Moving forward after pet loss is not about forgetting but about integrating the past into a new narrative, embracing new beginnings, and finding joy in the continuity of love.

In navigating the intricate landscapes of pet loss grief, these takeaways serve as guideposts, offering insights, compassion, and practical strategies to navigate the transformative healing journey.

In the tapestry of life, the love we share with our pets forms threads that weave through our hearts, leaving imprints that endure beyond time and space. As you navigate the path of pet loss grief, remember that healing is a gentle journey, and remembrance is a tribute to the enduring bonds that shape our lives.

In the quiet moments when the ache of loss lingers, may you find solace in the memories—the laughter, the pawprints on your heart, and the shared moments that etch themselves into the tapestry of your soul. Embrace the tears, for they are the gentle rain that nurtures the garden of love you cultivated together.

Know that grief is not a linear path but a mosaic of emotions; each piece is a testament to the depth of your connection. In the quiet corners of your heart, your beloved pet's spirit lives on—in the echoes of their presence, the warmth of shared memories, and the love that transcends the realms of the tangible.

As you embark on the journey of healing, may the stories of others, the comfort of shared experiences, and the enduring threads of love be your companions. Let your pet's legacy be a source of inspiration, guiding you toward new beginnings, fresh connections, and the promise of joy yet to be discovered.

Parting is not an end but a transformation—a dance between the pain of loss and the beauty of remembrance. May your heart find comfort in the knowledge that the love you shared is a timeless melody, playing softly in the background of your life, a constant reminder that the bonds forged with our pets are unbreakable, even by the hands of time.

In the tender embrace of remembrance and the promise of healing, may you find the strength to cherish the past, live fully in the present, and welcome future possibilities. The journey continues, and with each step, may your heart find peace, your soul find solace, and the love you shared with your beloved pet be an eternal flame that guides you on your way.

If you need additional resources for managing grief related to pet loss, consider the following options:

- Grief counseling services specializing in pet loss grief

- Online community forums

- Bereavement support groups

- Blogs

- Books on grief

- Social media groups dedicated to grief support

Remember, seeking support is a courageous step towards healing. Each person's grief journey is unique, and finding the resources that resonate with you is essential. Whether through professional counseling, community forums, or literature, may these resources provide comfort and understanding as you navigate the path of pet loss grief.